PRAISE FOR *MAKING THE NEWS*

"Salzman gives you the nitty-gritty, the nuts and bolts, to compete in the not-so-free marketplace of ideas."
   —**Matthew Rothschild, Editor,** *The Progressive*

"Salzman understands what it's like to be a small nonprofit with no staff to do media and little or no front money to finance events."
   —*Grassroots Fundraising Journal*

"Marvelous. A great handbook for activists."
   —**Jeff Cohen, Executive Director,**
   Fairness and Accuracy in Reporting

"An excellent edition to the required reading for many public relations courses."
   —*Journalism Educator*

"I wish Jason Salzman would stop giving away our secrets."
   —**Dick Kreck, Columnist,** *Denver Post*

"An extremely useful and informative book that provides everything an activist needs to know for communicating effectively through the media."
   —**David Cortright, President, Fourth Freedom Forum**

"The best book available for learning how to define and deliver messages that make news—and a difference."
   —**Bill Walker, California Director, Environmental Working Group**

"Even if you don't do media work, Salzman's *Making the News* is a great read that will help you understand what becomes news and how it got there."
   —**Brian Smith,** *In Brief,* **Earthjustice Legal Defense Fund**

"Given the book's simply style and lack of unnecessary detail, nonprofit organizations and activists alike would benefit from reading *Making the News*."
   —*Journal of International Law and Politics*

MAKING THE NEWS

A Guide for
Activists and Nonprofits

Revised and Updated

JASON SALZMAN

A Member of the Perseus Books Group

Copyright © 2003 by Westview Press, A Member of the Perseus Books Group

Westview Press books are available at special discounts for bulk purchases in the United States by corporations, institutions, and other organizations. For more information, please contact the Special Markets Department at the Perseus Books Group, 11 Cambridge Center, Cambridge MA 02142, or call (617) 252-5298 or (800) 255-1514 or email j.mccrary@perseusbooks.com.

Published in the United States of America by Westview Press, 5500 Central Avenue, Boulder, Colorado 80301–2877 and in the United Kingdom by Westview Press, 12 Hid's Copse Road, Cumnor Hill, Oxford OX2 9JJ.

Find us on the World Wide Web at www.westviewpress.com

A Cataloging-in-Publication data record for this book is available from the Library of Congress.

ISBN 0-8133-4095-0

The paper used in this publication meets the requirements of the American National Standard for Permanence of Paper for Printed Library Materials Z39.48–1984.

10   9   8   7   6   5   4   3   2   1

Contents

Acknowledgments

IF YOU ARE AN ACTIVIST or nonprofit professional, this book is dedicated to you. You probably deserve more recognition than you get. But here's the catch: Now that you've got a media book dedicated to you, you are obliged to make media relations more of a priority in your work.

I'd also like to dedicate *Making the News* to my wife, Anne, and my parents, Manny and Joanne.

My colleagues at Rocky Mountain Media Watch, including Andy Bardwell, John Boak, Barb Donachy, the late Paul Klite, Tory Read, and Kate Reinisch, helped get the book off the ground. We share the belief that if journalists are going to do a good job, they need to hear from citizens with story ideas. Without Aaron Toso's assistance, writing this second edition would have been much less fun and more time consuming. Thanks to former librarian Jane Button, who ably read the manuscript for typos even though she thought the guerrilla tactics described in the book are "underhanded and sneaky, offensive and obnoxious, destructive and irresponsible, and dirty and costly."

Leo Wiegman, my first editor at Westview Press, accepted my manuscript after my file of rejection letters was bulging. I am thankful to both Leo and my current Westview editor, Steve Catalano, for their help.

Thanks to all the journalists who let me interview them for this book. Not only did most journalists I called readily accept my request for an interview but they wanted to do it immediately—so as not to drag out the distraction from their work. Writing this book reminded me again how many committed, conscientious people work for news organizations. But it also brought to light the difficult conditions most journalists face at their jobs, particularly as staffs shrink and ownership of major news outlets is concentrated in the hands of a smaller and smaller number of large corporations.

I would also like to thank these nonprofit professionals and activists: Nadine Bloch, Robert Bray, Twilly Cannon, John Carr, Tom Clements, Ben Cohen, Gary Ferdman, Art Goodtimes, Andrew Greenblatt, Claire Greensfelder, David Grinspoon, Don Hancock, Peggy Huppert, David Lewis, Rich Male, Bob McFarland, Jack Mento, Chris Miller, Damon Moglen, LeRoy Moore, Duane Peterson, Jan Pilcher, Tom Rauch, Dan Reicher, Doug Richardson, Mike Roselle, Jacob Scherr, Mag and Ken Seaman, George Seidel, John Sellers, Shannon Service, Jack Shanahan, Richard Steckel, Mark Stevens, Susan Stroud, Chet Tchozewski, Bill Walker, Bill Walsh, Ralph Walsh, Harold Ward, Harvey Wasserman, and Robin Weingarten.

Finally, thanks to my son, Dylan, who never stops. And my daughter, Nell, who never sleeps.

Jason Salzman
Denver, Colorado

P.S. E-mail ideas or feedback to jason@causecommunications.com.

Introduction:
Let the World Know

IF YOU'RE LIKE MOST ACTIVISTS or nonprofit staffers, you've got a good cause but your media program—if you've got one—is a classic snoozer, lacking the imagery, humor, conflict, and celebrity appeal that make news.

Would you dress in a pink ostrich costume and tell politicians to get their heads out of the sand? Or, if you were kicked out of a mall for breast-feeding, would you fight back and stage a "breast-feed-in" with forty nursing moms—and the media—in tow?

Even if you advocated vegetarianism, would you ever lob a letter to Oklahoma City bomber Timothy McVeigh asking him to choose a meatless meal as his last supper prior to his execution—a move that generated major media attention?

If you opposed the Iraq war, would you find forty-nine other people, strip naked, and spell "peace" with your bodies? Would you deliver manure to politicians and tell them they are full of !!**@??!!.

You probably wouldn't, but this is exactly how you need to start *thinking* to upgrade your media profile.

True, you must have a firm grip on media basics (like deadlines, interviews, and follow-up calls to reporters) to make news, and your communications goals and strategy should be clear. But you also need to nurture a war-room attitude, infused with creativity, which is the soul of effective media work.

This book will help you do both—be strategic *and* creative when it comes to the media.

1

Saving the World in Obscurity?

On tight budgets, activists and nonprofit staffers often argue that trying to get media attention distracts them from doing the *real* work—managing programs, organizing, fund-raising, recruiting volunteers, and so on.

So they are left struggling to save the world in the dim light of obscurity and wondering why more people don't value what they do. And worse, they never benefit from all the ways that getting media coverage can make their work easier.

When they try to capture the media's attention, the "media events" that they organize are often so boring that even the most sympathetic editors cannot include them in today's competitive entertainment-oriented news "shows" or in the newspaper. For example, protesters in Nevada complain that they receive scant news coverage of their rallies at a former testing site for nuclear bombs near Las Vegas. Yet protests are so common there that the government has placed a permanent sign near the gate: DEMON-STRATORS ON ROADWAY. If you were an editor, how would you rate the news value of a rally near that sign? Admirable commitment to a cause, yes. Comedy, maybe. News, no.

If it's media attention you want—and it's clearly media attention you *need* in order to communicate to mass audiences—then you should learn how to be successful at attracting journalists to your cause. For many activists like me, this comes with a price: An effective media strategy requires a willingness to cater to the often-warped priorities and short attention span of the news media.

This book has all the information you need to publicize your cause in the local, national, and international news media. It's written specifically for activists, nonprofit groups, or any concerned citizen who doesn't have a big advertising budget but wants to get the word out.

I know from firsthand experience how busy the activists and staff at nonprofit organizations are. I understand how frustrating it is to pick up a book that's supposed to contain a few tips I can actually use in my day-to-day work only to find that it's been written by a theorist who's completely disconnected to my real-world needs.

This book, in contrast, was written for people who don't have time to read about how to change the world but have to figure

Frequent demonstrations forced officials to erect this sign. Would you expect a rally here to make the news? You'll break into the news by being creative. CREDIT: JASON SALZMAN

out how to do it anyway. It's designed to be *used*—free of unnecessary jargon or theory and easy to understand. Its detailed index and table of contents allow you to access information quickly without having to read entire chapters, much less the entire book.

For example, if you're scheduled for a talk-radio show tomorrow, turn to Chapter 28 for tips on how to prepare. If you want information on how to publish a letter to the editor in the newspaper, look at Chapter 24. Need to stage a media event or stunt? See the step-by-step instructions in Part Three. Tired of the traditional approach and want to go for guerrilla media? Flip to Part Six, "Prime-Time Guerrilla Activism." Confused about Internet bloggers, viral marketing, and the latest PR on the Web? Read Part Five, "Your Cause in Cyberspace." It's all concise and user-friendly.

This second edition is completely updated to help you compete in the Internet age.

Inside-the-Media Insights from Journalists

Many people seem to think news is gathered and written by an amorphous power dispensing copy via the News God—who promotes greed and evil at the expense of real people and their interests. The truth is that news organizations are composed of people, a lot of whom want to talk to you and are trying to do a good job even as their employment is threatened by corporate mergers and changes in communications technologies.

Throughout this book, you'll find quotes from professional journalists. They offer their inside-the-media insights on how to put your cause on the airwaves and in print. Their comments, coupled with advice from activists, demystify the news and the news-gathering process.

Ethical Spin

I don't think activists and community groups need new ideas to save the world—though I wish for great ideas anyway. We just have to communicate old ideas more effectively. We need to focus on packaging, just like big corporations and politicians do.

Look at what the George W. Bush administration did when it wanted to invade Iraq. It developed a meticulous marketing plan, which explained that Bush should not call for war during the summer. Why? For national security reasons? No. Because "from a marketing point of view, you don't introduce new products in August," according to White House Chief of Staff Andrew Card, quoted in the *New York Times*. The communications strategy called for President Bush to begin marketing the Iraq war in his speech on the anniversary of the World Trade Center attacks—a speech that everyone knew would grab headlines. The plan went on from there.

Your spokesperson may not be the president, but you can use the media strategically, too.

It may sound hollow and slimy to advocate, in effect, fighting spin with spin. But "spin" simply refers to promoting your best argument forward, with a "war room" if you've got one.

What matters is the integrity of the "spinner." If you work for Monsanto and you claim that a toxic chemical is safe when it's not, you are hollow and slimy and you should quit. Likewise, if you work for Greenpeace and you lie about the environmental effects of a pesticide, you should change your ways or find something else to do. We spinners have to constantly check in with our hearts and ensure that we're doing the right thing. As long as you maintain your integrity, doing public relations is as honorable as any type of work. PR is nothing to be ashamed of.

This book will help you develop the skills and strategy you'll need to succeed *over the long haul*. It will enable you to compete with foes who've got war chests that dwarf your tiny budget. With your commitment to changing the direction of our society as your foundation, you can begin building a great communications program today.

Part ONE

Stop Being a Bore

"THE MOST IMAGINATIVE AND THEATRICAL people are going to win," says Colin Covert, a feature reporter at the *Star Tribune* in Minneapolis. "Don't expect good intentions to get you space. The fact that you're trying to fight cancer is great, but it's not news. If you do something interesting, we'll write about it."

It's easy to complain about mayhem and fluff in the news. And it's convenient to blame journalists for *not* covering issues and causes—stories that might help solve the problems our society faces.

But the truth is, every citizen shares the blame with the news media. We do not offer journalists enough opportunities—in the right packaging and at the right time—to cover causes and important issues.

This section is intended to help you to think not just outside the box about your media work—but outside the stratosphere. It will help you create symbols and imagery that will carry your cause into the news.

1

Think Outside
the Stratosphere

SUCCESSFUL MEDIA CAMPAIGNS ARE, above all else, *entertaining*. That doesn't necessarily mean *amusing*. In fact, some successful media campaigns are disgusting. But whether amusing or disgusting—they are *engaging*, and that is the key synonym for entertainment in the news business.

This chapter shows how activists creatively manipulate the media. It's meant to inspire you to break free from the standard ways of communicating about causes.

I've divided creative media tactics—both outrageous and banal—into categories, each followed by bite-sized samples. For example, the first category is simply to use a costume, and below it are specific examples of how advocates have used costumes to make news.

WAYS TO GET MEDIA ATTENTION
Cameras Love Costumes

In this age of theatrical "news" shows, it's easy to understand why costumes are a great tool to attract news cameras. They can be humorous, bright, lively, confrontational—all characteristics of a newsworthy event. Even a simple mask can get you on the evening news.

Your Head Is in the Sand

"Every time we have someone dress in this stupid pink ostrich costume, it gets media attention," says Dan Cantor, director of New York's Working Families Party, which dressed an activist as an ostrich to illustrate how various politicians (like New York's mayor) have their "heads in the sand" over various issues (like the economy). "It's so ridiculously effective, it's depressing. We do lots and lots of serious work, and this is what draws the cameras."

"Pigs" Oppose Pork-Barrel Politics

Federal spending for projects that are not truly needed but maintained to provide jobs is called "pork-barrel" spending. At Greenpeace in Colorado, we had no tolerance for politicians who refused to call for the shutdown of unsafe nuclear-bomb making at the nearby Rocky Flats plant simply because the plant provided jobs. How did we make the point? Three activists dressed in larger-than-life fuzzy pig costumes that were rented from a costume shop. A dozen others donned simple rubber pig noses, which would have been fine by themselves. They snorted around in front of television cameras outside a dark auditorium where a not-made-for-TV hearing about Rocky Flats was taking place.

Santa Claus Testifies

In Indianapolis, Indiana, citizens were upset over the high utility rates set by the Public Utilities Commission. They wanted the public to understand that the commission was allowing power companies to make huge profits at its expense. So during a July public hearing, Santa Claus showed up. "He walked into the hearing room and sat down right next to the commissioners," says organizer David Culp. "It brought the whole thing to a screeching halt. People did not know what to do." The message as reported by the media: The commissioners were being Santa Claus to private power companies by allowing them to charge high rates.

Rather than simply carrying a sign decrying pork-barrel spending on nuclear bomb production, these activists attracted the news media with pig costumes. CREDIT: JASON SALZMAN

More Costumes: Eyeballs, Killer Tomatoes, Lemons, Gags, and Animals

Activists have dressed as eyeballs (voters are watching as you make a decision), killer tomatoes (stop genetically modified crops), hazardous-waste workers (beware of a toxic danger), bears carrying "Homeless" signs (stop clear-cutting), lemons ("nukes are sour, wind is power"), and almost anything else you can think of. A gag across the mouth creates a visual image of citizens being excluded from a debate or silenced for whatever reason. Animals strike a responsive chord among people.

Dramatize a Popular Expression or Word

When you dramatize expressions with props and costumes, you can create ironic humor and conflict that make news. The key is to think of an expression, cliché, word, or idiom that both describes the essential message of your event *and* lends itself to being acted out or somehow made literal. Sometimes the phrase you're looking for is right in front of you because you use it every time you talk about your issue (for example, "I know the governor's in bed with them!").

In Bed with Polluters

It was clear to activists in Arizona that officials from the state's environmental agencies were ignoring their concerns because of their cozy relationship with a large company proposing to build an incinerator in the state. To make this point to the public, they put the government agencies in bed with the polluters, literally. They hauled a bed to the steps of the state capitol, put effigies of the polluters and the officials in it, and announced they would remain there "until the government gets out of bed with polluters." Fake money streamed out of the pockets of the "polluters," and the protesters used giant blowups of dollar bills as backdrops. Other signs read "Why are government agencies in bed with the polluters?" During the seven-day protest, the activists generated major local coverage, including live telecasts and daily updates from "The Bed." Sound bites:

"The government isn't even taking precautions" and "Politics makes for strange bedfellows, but the adage has never been demonstrated more explicitly."

Waffling on the Issues

In a display of creativity on the campaign trail, one candidate in a congressional race held a press conference in front of a waffle house to dramatize the point that his opponent was "waffling on the issues."

Clowns, Red Tape, Chickens, Ostriches, Steamrollers, and Bullshit

AIDS activists, critical of the federal government's long process for analyzing drugs before they were released to the public, wrapped themselves in red tape to illustrate that government "red tape" was costing lives. Planned Parenthood activists dropped Alka-Seltzer into a glass of water to show that antiabortion protests had "fizzled." Activists have dressed as chickens to illustrate that a politician is too "chicken" to take on a tough issue. They rented a tree shredder, the kind used by tree-trimming companies to shred branches, to illustrate that international trade agreements would "shred" environmental laws. They threw mock "laws" in a trash can to illustrate how international agreements would "trash" labor laws. Critics of Star Wars held a news conference under a leaky umbrella, illustrating how the missile defense system would "leak." Democrats rented an actual steamroller to show voters that Republicans were "steamrolling" their tax proposals through Congress. Activists created a giant "Band-Aid" to illustrate how politicians were applying Band-Aids, rather than solving problems. Clowns or monkeys can be used to implore politicians to stop "clowning" or "monkeying" around in the legislature. A gift of a "Backbone" shows spinelessness. A "first aid kit" can be offered to a good politician who was "beaten up" by a bad one. "Fudge" can be used to show how a politician is "fudging the numbers." Alarm clocks send a "wake-up call" to politicians. Rabbits show that citizens are "hopping mad." Ostriches tell a politician to get his or her head out of the sand. Skunks say that a decision or policy "stinks." Finally, environmental activists thought Sen. Dianne Feinstein's compromise on a logging issue was "bullshit." Guess what they dumped in front of her office.

Use Live Animals

Think of all the "news" you've seen about the stuck cat, the runaway parrot, Skippy the squirrel, or the lost bear. *Live* animals are newsworthy. They excel at being cute and unpredictable—

and have universal interest. You just have to think of a way to connect a live animal, preferably a manageable one, to your cause. But beware; you may attract protests from animal-rights groups, especially if you don't handle your live beings with care—which you should do. You will have to decide whether possible protests and ensuing media coverage caused by animal-rights activists will help or hurt you.

Blessing of the Pets

"For the most part, they were a sacrilegious bunch. They barked during the blessing. They lifted their legs instead of saying 'amen.'" So began an article in the *Athens Daily News* about "blessing of the animals" day at the Catholic Center at the University of Georgia. It turns out that many churches across the country conduct similar blessings, in honor of the animal-loving St. Francis—who would have certainly been in PR had he not lived in the early 1200s.

Paying Utility Bills in Chickens

Residents of a semi-rural area in Portland, Oregon, faced high utility bills, partly for services they did not receive. The people weren't rich, but they did have chickens. So to highlight the unfair utility charges, they tried to pay their bills in pennies, chickens, and the shirts off their backs. One local TV station covered the stunt live, as security guards told the citizens that no chickens were allowed in city buildings.

Percy the Dog for Congress

As a protest against politics-as-usual, Wayne Genthner entered his border collie, Percy, into a Florida congressional race. The dog's supporters included people standing on street corners wearing sandwich boards in support of Percy for Congress. The media lapped up the story.

Zoos have the perfect live-in props for media events. In this case, the Denver Zoo made news by celebrating a polar bear's birthday with a stinky cake and fish candle. CREDIT: JOHN PRIETO, DENVER POST

More Animals in the News

Notice how the police always trot out their latest sniffer for the cameras. Sheep farmers in France brought 250 of their animals to a demonstration to protest rising fuel prices, generating worldwide coverage. Ditto with the British poultry farmers who trucked hens to their rally against so-called free trade agreements. White doves are a newsworthy symbol of peace. (See "Dramatize a Popular Expression or Word" above for more animal ideas.)

The Worst or the Best: Give an Award

The media love winners and losers. The bigger, the better. What better way to illustrate that someone's a total failure than to give him or her an "F" or an award for being despicable? Conversely, an opportunity for a photo of a politician receiving flowers for outstanding behavior may be hard for the news media to pass up. And it's the type of image the public tends to remember.

The Dirty Dozen

Every other year, the League of Conservation Voters inducts twelve members of Congress into an elite club: the Dirty Dozen. These lawmakers are, in the League of Conservation Voters' opinion, the most offensive enemies of the environment to (dis)grace the halls of Congress. The league consistently generates news coverage from this award, which is strategically announced before an election, giving voters the opportunity to dump the dirty dozen from office.

Report Card for the Energy Secretary

In an effort to draw attention to the poor performance of Energy Secretary James Watkins, the Military Production Network, a national alliance of citizens' organizations, presented him with a "report card." The network invited the news media to witness the presentation of the report card, which appeared in the *Washington Post* with this quote from Idaho organizer Liz Paul: "If I came home with that report card, I'd have been grounded for the summer, had my allowance cut, and had the car keys taken away."

A Ticket, Flowers, and More Awards

Activists have presented flowers to the French ambassador after France announced a moratorium on nuclear testing; "gas-guzzling violations" to low-mileage cars; an annual "burned-out light bulb" award to a legislator; and Valentine's Day gifts to favorite public servants.

Make the Most of a Petition

Some activists collect signatures to put an issue on the election ballot. These petitions are meticulously counted and regulated according to election rules. Undertaking a ballot initiative is a major campaign, and the formal presentation of the required signatures, usually to the secretary of state's office, is often noted by the media.

Most activists, however, circulate petitions simply to draw attention to a problem. Unfortunately, after arriving in a politician's mailbox, these petitions often go straight into the trash can or, if we're lucky, the recycling bin.

Petitions should be delivered in a way that creates an image and drama for the news media.

A Petition Carpet

Greenpeace activists collected over 100,000 signatures to pressure the government to stop nuclear weapons production. It was my job to decide how to attract media attention to the presentation of the petitions. I decided to create a carpet by taping the letter-sized petitions onto cheap burlap fabric.

We stretched the carpet from the governor of Colorado's car to the doors of the state capitol. An insider gave us a tip that the governor would be going to his car at a certain hour, and we hoped he would step on our "carpet," illustrating our point that he was "trampling on the will of the people" by not calling for the shutdown of nuclear-bomb production. Instead, the governor's press secretary greeted us and a handful of photographers.

I thought she would have enough media savvy not to step on the petition carpet, but she plunked her foot right down on it. Her photo was on the front page of one local newspaper.

A Petition Roll

The AFL-CIO obtained hundreds of signatures on a thirty-six-inch-wide roll of paper, which was unfurled on the Capitol steps in Washington, D.C. An Associated Press photo of it appeared in papers across the United States.

More Petition Ideas

Deliver petitions inside something (for example, a coffin, trash can, or symbol of your issue) or have your petition focus on some other body besides the government (perhaps a hospital, senior center, school, or chamber of commerce). You can also write creative petition questions that may be more newsworthy. Instead of quietly delivering petitions to politicians, pro-choice activists from Kansas City received substantial media coverage by simply draping taped petitions over the railings of the U.S. Capitol rotunda. Environmental activists, led by the Public Interest Research Group, stuffed thousands of petitions in cloth bags and assembled them on the steps of the Capitol, generating a national AP photo. And gay activists created a petition wall at a rally, allowing protesters to stop by the wall—which created a great action photo.

Make a Banner

Banners have been dropped from every kind of structure in support of every conceivable cause. A banner unveiled at the right moment in the right place can generate a lot of attention in most media markets, even though this tactic has been used repeatedly. When all else fails, you don't even need a banner. Hold up a large sign. Never underestimate the power of signs as news, especially if the timing is right.

"Next Time . . . Try Recycling"

On a cold September morning, a garbage barge crept out of New York Harbor and embarked on an eleven-month worldwide search for a dumpsite for its cargo of household waste. As each government rejected the barge, the international media frenzy

Greenpeace targeted a garbage barge to focus the attention of the news media on the need for recycling.
Credit: Greenpeace/Dennis Capalongo

around it grew. By the time the barge returned to New York, it had become the object of a full-court international media event. It had become a symbol of the "garbage problem." As it floated in New York Harbor, waiting for instructions on what to do next, two Greenpeace activists swam out to it with a banner. The media were notified, and with photographers assembled, the activists unveiled the banner against the backdrop of garbage: "Next Time . . . Try Recycling." The photo of this event became an instant worldwide media hit.

AIDS Memorial Quilt

The AIDS Memorial Quilt is a beautiful media hit that can easily be adapted for another cause. Each panel of the quilt represents someone who died of AIDS, and it had about 2,000 panels when it was first displayed on the Mall in Washington, D.C., in 1987. Sections of the quilt, which now has over 45,000 panels, are displayed periodically and continue to be a media draw—a powerful visual representation of a horrible disease and the need to find a cure for it.

More Banner Ideas

Activists have dropped banners from construction sites, churches, and state capitols; put letters on people's shirts (one letter per shirt), making a human banner; and placed photos of women who have had breast cancer on a banner.

Stage a Roadside Protest and Call Traffic Reporters

Radio audiences are at their peak during morning and evening rush hours, and traffic reports are a fixture on most popular radio stations during these hours. If you can somehow inject your message into the traffic reports, you will reach a huge radio audience. It turns out that this is not as difficult as you might think. Traffic reports, you will notice, frequently broadcast traffic problems phoned in by drivers. If you create a traffic-related "problem," which actually may not disrupt traffic at all, you can worm your way into the traffic reports. How to do it? Stage a protest by the side of the highway and call the traffic reporters. This works. As one veteran radio reporter told me, "If you're climbing a billboard along the highway, people will call us on their cell phones."

One Friday morning, ten freeway overpasses in southern California carried more than commuter traffic: Banners were slung on the overpasses, facing the freeway below, protesting Governor Pete Wilson's proposal to construct a waste dump in southern California. The banners read, "Wilson: Stop Your Nuclear Dump." The protest received widespread attention because the traffic reports on the morning radio shows announced the presence of the banners repeatedly, in part because activists and drivers with cell phones made sure the radio stations knew about them. Activists estimate that they reached millions of people in southern California that morning.

Create a Replica of the Problem (or the Solution)

Many political problems remain unsolved because the public literally can't see them. If problems become visible—and accessible to photographers and the media—the political will to solve them is much more likely to materialize.

Recognizing this, activists find ways to move social ills from behind locked doors into the public domain—into our communal backyard. One way to do this is to create a replica of the problem. The following media events involve realistic replicas, larger-than-life replicas, or replicas of disasters.

The Nuclear Arsenal in Clay

After viewing artist Barbara Donachy's 34,000 miniature clay bombs and submarines representing the entire U.S. nuclear arsenal, a teacher told Donachy: "Wow, I thought we only had 100 bombs. It's good to have something like this so people know." Designed to present a realistic visual image of U.S. nuclear weaponry, the display was shown across this country and abroad during the height of the Cold War. The mottled patterns of the cones and their shadows covering 5,000 square feet inspired the name *Amber Waves of Grain*. The piece is now permanently displayed at the National Peace Museum in Nebraska.

Mock Nuclear-Waste Cask

For years, activists in Nevada struggled to expand public opposition to the proposed Yucca Mountain nuclear waste dump near Las Vegas. The dump would hold radioactive waste from nuclear reactors across the United States. They decided to draw wider attention to the problem by highlighting the highways on which the waste would be transported to Nevada. To do this, they built a full-sized, mock transport cask. They trucked it to rallies and toured around the United States with it, generating news coverage at most stops.

Shanty Towns and Animals

Students opposing apartheid in South Africa constructed "shanty towns" in public places to depict living conditions for blacks in South Africa. Animal-rights groups have created papier-mâché animals to draw attention to their demonstrations.

A 34,000-piece replica of the U.S. nuclear arsenal, composed of miniature clay bombs and submarines, generated international news coverage.
CREDIT: BARBARA DONACHY

A Re-enacted Second Marriage

The Rev. Jimmy Creech faced suspension by the United Methodist ministry. The reason: He had presided over the marriage ceremony of two gay men. The day before the trial, Creech exposed his crime to the world by re-enacting the wedding of the two gay men, in front of national media.

A Giant Radioactive-Waste Barrel

I try to figure out how low-budget variations of expensive advertising tricks can work for nonprofit organizations. Once I was skiing and was slightly depressed to see a giant beer can with a radio station's name on it nestled in the trees below the chairlift. The twenty-foot inflatable beer can was just like the ones you see at street fairs, but it looked uglier in the forest—even if it was on the side of a ski slope. In any case, I saw the giant can and said to myself, "Maybe Greenpeace can get one of those." I checked around and found out that custom-made, they were $5,000 or more. I eventually found a Greenpeace volunteer who had worked for one of the companies that manufacture these inflatables. She made us a twenty-foot-tall "inflatable radioactive waste barrel." It was radioactive yellow with a black-and-white radiation symbol painted on it. Every time we faced a fight over radioactive waste, we hauled out the giant barrel, "dumping" it on the capitol steps in different cities. And nearly every time, it was a media hit, generating huge amounts of free publicity.

Exploding Nuclear Reactor

Activists in South Carolina created a ten-foot-high nuclear reactor equipped with a siren and fire extinguisher for mock explosions to demonstrate the danger posed by nuclear reactors at the Savannah River nuclear-bomb plant.

Depict a Symbol of Your Concerns

A variation on replicating the problem is to create a visual representation of the issue you are working on.

Certificate of Dropping Out

Principal Joseph Sandoval was concerned about the high drop-out rate at his high school. To generate debate about the problem—and to send a message to students who might leave school—he presented dropouts with a "certificate of dropping out." The stunt got national media attention.

Gun Victims' Shoes

Shootings and killings are ubiquitous in the news, particularly on local television news. But how often do you see protests about guns? And if you do, how often do they make an impact that lasts? The Coalition to Stop Gun Violence searched for a symbol that could pierce the numbness many of us have developed about violent crime. It assembled 40,000 pairs of shoes of citizens killed by guns. A rally in Washington, D.C., might not have generated any coverage, but this creative protest on the Washington Mall got national attention.

Empty Chairs, Memorial Roadside Signs, and Silhouettes

University students assembled 100 empty chairs on the campus lawn, symbolizing the 100 students who were denied admission due to lack of financial aid; community activists invited officials to play "Pin the Tail on the Rat" in a park infested with, you guessed it, rats; neighbors responded to anti-Semitic activities by placing menorahs in their windows; and domestic-violence opponents marked Domestic-Violence Prevention Month by placing cardboard silhouettes of fifty domestic-violence victims on the Colorado capitol lawn.

Expose the Actual Problem

Rather than expose a symbol of the problem you face, you can expose or reveal the actual problem in a public place. Here are some examples of how activists successfully exposed real problems.

Crawling for Access

As part of their campaign to obtain access to the Colorado capitol, activists for organizations representing people with disabilities decided they would expose the problem. Because there was insufficient wheelchair access, they abandoned their wheelchairs and tried to crawl up the steps of the capitol with a throng of TV cameras in tow. On the backs of their shirts, they wrote, "Why must we crawl?" At the time they staged their protest, the legislature was considering a bill to provide funds to modify the capitol for access.

Lemonade with a Twist

"Would you or any members of your court like a drink?" asked Radford Lyons, age eight, at a public hearing. He then offered the hearing officials free lemonade made from contaminated well water in Pike County, Kentucky. The protest was part of a campaign by Kentuckians for the Commonwealth to have water lines extended to homes in the area of the contaminated wells. At the end of the hearing, one official promised to have the water lines constructed.

Other Problems Exposed

Janitors brought three toilets, a brush, a stopwatch, and five dollars to a city council meeting—and challenged council members to make a living cleaning bathrooms under the current minimum wage. Supporters of a ban on land mines piled their prosthetic devices in front of the White House. Wind-power proponents dumped a ton of coal, the amount used by an average home in two months, in front of the Boulder County Courthouse. Mothers Against Drunk Driving sponsored a news conference with a wheelchair-bound woman, against the backdrop of her mangled car, hit by a drunk driver.

Vote on It

A vote is a great way to transform an idea into an event that can be covered by the media. Not only does a vote clearly identify winners and losers for journalists, it also adds credibility to "fringe" positions. Voting is a respectable, thoroughly accepted way to decide any question. A vote of an entire town or state is of obvious news value, but even a ballot question put before a church or temple, school, civic group, or senior center can be newsworthy. For example, a petition with 100 signatures has less news value than a vote of 100 members of a church.

"Suicide Pills" for Use After Nuclear War

When I was a student at Brown University in 1982, the threat of nuclear war was at its peak. Members of the Reagan administration

Seated in a wheelchair in front of a car severely damaged in a crash,
survivor Artis Selby advocates wearing seat belts at a news conference.
Credit: Glen Asakawa, Denver Post.

openly talked about fighting and winning a nuclear battle. Meanwhile, the antinuclear movement, which had gained national momentum around the idea of freezing the arms race, had begun to decline. I didn't understand how this could be so. The only explanation I could come up with was that the possibility of nuclear war was too abstract for people to understand. This meant that we antinuclear activists had the challenge of bringing the problem home somehow.

Looking around the campus, I observed that signs identified dormitory basements as fallout shelters for use by students during nuclear war. I phoned the Federal Emergency Management Agency in downtown Providence, and it confirmed that the fallout shelters in the dorms were still part of the nation's defense against nuclear attack. As part of my activities with the Brown Disarmament Group, I led a petition drive calling on university president Howard Swearer to declare the fallout shelters useless for nuclear-war survival. Think about it: Could students survive a nuclear war in a dorm basement? Despite 1,000 student signatures, Swearer refused to make this declaration, telling me that he would consider the move if other Ivy League schools joined Brown. This was totally absurd, but what could I do? Most of my fellow disarmament activists thought that focusing on fallout shelters was a waste of time anyway. So I gave up and pursued another course: During the fallout shelter campaign, one student told me she'd prefer to have a suicide pill than hide in a fallout shelter. Though it sounds sort of crazy, this made sense to me. So some friends and I formed a new group, Students for Suicide Tablets. Our group collected 700 signatures to put the following item on the student council election ballot: "We, the undergraduate students of Brown University, request that Brown University Health Services stockpile suicide pills for optional student use exclusively in the event of a nuclear war." Once the measure was on the ballot, it was picked up by the *Providence Journal*, which learned about it from the *Brown Daily Herald*. The following day, the Associated Press called about the story, and by noon CBS News was on campus. Soon, we had spoken to journalists from most major media outlets in the United States. We were even guests on the Phil Donahue show.

In the following weeks on campus, students debated how they should vote on the suicide-pill measure. Most of the 700 students who had originally signed the suicide-pill petition, allowing the question to appear on the ballot, did so not because they wanted the pills but because they agreed that there was no harm in letting students vote on it. Initially, there was little support for the pills on campus. In fact, many heard about the issue only when fearful parents called to ask about the problem at school.

The director of Student Health Services, Dr. Sumner Hoffman, unwittingly stoked the already intense media frenzy around the upcoming vote by declaring his opposition to it: "Our mission is to sustain life, to improve the quality of life, to treat illness, not to destroy life." The university's spokesperson simply said, "No pills." He also tried to explain that he believed the students were motivated by "serious concerns" about nuclear war. Most students agreed and accepted the suicide pills as a symbol even though our group said the pills were both a symbol and a real request. In the end, students voted 60–40 percent for the pills. The results were announced by Dan Rather that evening. Brown never stocked the pills.

More Votes

In the months leading up to the Iraq war, 150 city councils across the United States voted to oppose a preemptive war against Iraq. Though the resolutions obviously had no legal force, they generated widespread and powerful publicity. Similarly, activists in the 1980s first drew attention to their proposal to freeze the production of nuclear weapons by staging referendums at places of worship, colleges, and town meetings in small New England towns. Eventually, entire states voted to "freeze the nuclear arms race."

Get Naked—Or at Least Partially

Titillation is one of the hallmarks of news. So, you'd expect nakedness to get press, and it does. The more skin exposed, the better—to a point. While presenting the naked truth, you want to be tasteful. (Incidentally, inspired by the film *The Full Monty*, I tried to find more examples of male nudity in the protest news, but could not. Let me know if you hear of any.)

Peace from Their Bodies

"I just thought, what can I do?" Donna Sheehan, 72, told the Associated Press. "What can we do? It's a desperate feeling. Well, this is what we did." Sheehan and forty-nine other northern California activists stripped naked and spelled the word "Peace" with their bodies, in opposition to the war with Iraq.

Bras for a Cause

I'm watching the TV news and there's a story all the way from London: a race to fight breast cancer. What makes this event, important as the cause is, international news? The 8,000 moonlight runners—both men and women—were clad in bras.

These anti-fur activists know that skin makes news.
PHOTOS TAKEN BY PETA.

Naked Cat in a Cage

People for the Ethical Treatment of Animals (PETA) alleges that the Ringling Brothers and Barnum & Bailey Circus treats its animals poorly. So PETA followed the circus from town to town. At each stop, a mostly naked PETA protester with tiger ears would sit inside a cage holding a sign, "Wild Animals Don't Belong Behind Bars."

Other Naked News

Four women got national news coverage for holding a "topless prayer vigil" against clear-cutting. Pro-choice women wore tank tops with the words, "Keep your laws off my body" printed on their bare stomachs. Similarly, in a campaign for vegetarianism, PETA drew lines on a woman's body corresponding to cuts of beef (such as, round, rib, shoulder). Finally, don't forget about streakers. They get a lot of attention.

Websites As News

The Web allows you to establish an organization in cyberspace in response to breaking news and quickly to become part of a breaking news story. Or you can build a Website around controversial or funny information and make news. Keep track of Website hits or other quantifiable evidence that your site is popular to convince reporters that your story is legit.

www.BillionairesForBushorGore.com

This "bipartisan coalition of rich donors," based in cyberspace, was created by United for a Fair Economy to highlight its position that wealthy donors control the agendas of both the Democratic and Republican parties. The "Vigil for Corporate Welfare" and "Million Billionaires March," which actually took place at the party conventions, received generous coverage. The Website anchored the organization.

www.campus-watch.org

This site, the brainchild of right-winger Daniel Pipes at the Middle East Forum, published "dossiers" of professors who allegedly had "left-leaning" views on Palestinian and Middle East issues. The site was attacked by outraged professors who saw it as an assault on free speech and an effort to intimidate academics who speak out against Israeli policies.

www.citizensunited.org

As celebrities were showered with media coverage for opposing the Iraq war, pro-war activists quickly set up this Website calling on citizens to ignore the anti-war voices in Hollywood. This Website rapidly became part of the debate about whether it was appropriate for celebrities to air opinions about the war.

www.Fuckedcompany.com

This site was established as dot-com companies began failing and workers and reporters were looking for information about which companies would fall next.

See Chapter 43, "Guerrilla Activists Hit Cyberspace," for more ideas.

A Celebrity Endorsement

Take advantage of our society's obsession with sports and Hollywood. Finding a sports star, celebrity, or notable person to endorse your cause or speak at your event can be difficult, but it's worth the effort. I've seen a celebrity join a cause and suddenly change everything. Support comes out of nowhere. Your position becomes credible.

"Celebrities help stories," says Jon Craig, deputy political editor of the *Daily Express* in London. "I'm sure interest groups know that. If you've got Arnold Schwarzenegger or somebody famous to back your campaign, it helps."

Eleven-Foot Ice Cream "Budget Pie"

Ben Cohen, co-founder of Ben and Jerry's, unveiled the ice cream pie with different colored frosting showing the major categories of spending in the federal budget. Over half of discretionary spending goes to the Pentagon. "I obviously love ice cream," Cohen said. "But this budget pie is giving America indigestion." In front of a pack of reporters and photographers, Cohen scooped ice cream from the Pentagon portion of the pie to the "environmental protection" section. (As one of the people responsible for the pie, I would advise against using a substance that melts. But we got lucky, and this worked great—and tasted good, too.)

Celebrity Arrests

You can up the ante by finding a celebrity who's willing to get arrested for the cause. For example, Cynthia Nixon, a star in *Sex in the City* who also has a child in the New York public schools, protested New York education cuts by getting arrested with other parents.

Make Your Advertisement News

It's usually not a good idea for a small nonprofit organization to buy paid advertisements. Ads cost too much, especially if they are repeated enough times to make a dent in the minds of your audience. A half-page ad in the *New York Times*, for example, costs tens of thousands of dollars. But paid ads do make sense if they create a controversy and therefore become news themselves, exponentially stretching your advertising dollar.

"Bob, I've Got Emphysema."

In the seventh year of its statewide antismoking campaign, the California Health Department decided to step up its advertising campaign. It sponsored a series of ads that left a trail of media coverage and debate in their wake. One billboard depicted what appeared to be "Marlboro Country." But instead, one of the Marlboro men was saying to the other, "Bob, I've got emphysema." Another hard-hitting TV ad showed a woman whose larynx, or voice box, was removed because of the effects of throat cancer. But she continues to smoke through a hole in her throat, and she does so in the television ad.

Iraq War TV Ads

Knowing that issue-oriented advertisements are often covered in the news if the issue addressed in the ads is *already* grabbing headlines, the Win Without War Coalition produced low-budget TV ads opposing the Iraq war just as President George W. Bush began pushing for war. The ads featured actress Susan Sarandon, comedian Janeane Garafalo, retired Vice Admiral Jack Shanahan, and former U.S. Ambassador to Iraq Edward Peck. Even though they appeared only on local cable outlets, the ads became national news, covered by national and local print media, network morning and evening news shows, cable talk shows, news services, and many others—all eager for copy and imagery about the ongoing war story. In many cases the ads were shown in their entirety on TV news shows.

Gamble Colorado

At Greenpeace, we placed an ad in the western edition of the *New York Times,* which is less expensive than other editions but still carries the credibility and "national" appeal of the *Times.* The ad, headlined "Gamble Colorado," lauded the virtues of a vacation in Colorado: "Colorado is waiting for you. In the winter, you'll find world-class skiing at numerous Rocky Mountain ski areas and snow-covered cross-country tracks. In the summer, the hiker and bicycle rider have plenty to do. Secluded trails and

Gamble Colorado

Colorado is waiting for you. In the winter, you'll find world-class skiing at numerous Rocky Mountain ski areas and snow-covered cross-country tracks. In the summer, the hiker and bicycle rider have plenty to do. Secluded trails and mountain peaks make a perfect get-away. The Colorado towns of Black Hawk and Central City allow tourists to try their luck at games of chance. And there is more. Coloradans are famous for their hospitality and concern for visitors. From gourmet Denver restaurants to remote bed-and-breakfast hotels, Colorado wants to make this year's vacation your best ever! Make your reservations today.

GREENPEACE
1021 PEARL STREET, SUITE 200
BOULDER, COLORADO 80302

WARNING: In 1992, the government plans to restart nuclear bomb production at the Rocky Flats Plant, located 20 miles from the Denver airport. But the plutonium plant violates certain environmental laws and does not meet all current safety standards, and there is no safe way to dispose of the dangerous radioactive waste piled up at Rocky Flats. If you care about Colorado — and especially if you plan to visit the Denver area — make sure Rocky Flats stays closed. Tell Colorado Gov. Roy Romer (303-866-2575) to oppose the restart of Rocky Flats.

A warning label similar to those found on cigarette packages made this mock tourist advertisement newsworthy.
CREDIT: GREENPEACE

mountain peaks make a perfect get-away. The Colorado towns of Black Hawk and Central City allow tourists to try their luck at games of chance." However, it included a warning label—like the ones on cigarette cartons—advising tourists that Colorado might be unsafe to visit because of the Rocky Flats nuclear-bomb plant: "WARNING: In 1992, the government plans to restart nuclear bomb production at the Rocky Flats Plant, located 20 miles from the Denver airport. But the plutonium plant violates certain environmental laws and does not meet all current safety standards, and there is no safe way to dispose of dangerous radioactive waste piled up at Rocky Flats. If you care about Colorado—and especially if you plan to visit the Denver area—make sure Rocky Flats stays closed. Tell Colorado Gov. Roy Romer (303–866–2575) to oppose the restart of Rocky Flats." The ad was reprinted (for free) on the news pages of local papers and national advertising magazines. It also appeared on TV.

More Ads

An ad placed by religious groups as Congress was debating clean air standards asked the simple question, "What would Jesus Drive?" and hit a national media nerve. Another newsworthy ad featured an actual photo of the chief executive officer of DuPont, who was blamed for contributing to ozone destruction. After the mayor of New York City acknowledged that he had smoked marijuana, activists ran an ad with a photo of the mayor, congratulating him for his "candor." Then there's the guy who simply wanted more people to begin "thinking about God." So he ran billboard advertisements reading, "Let's meet at my house Sunday before the game.–God" This got national media attention.

Get Your Ad Rejected

Another way to make news with your advertisement and avoid the high costs of actually placing ads is to develop an ad that you know will be rejected by media outlets. Then hold a press conference or distribute a news release lambasting the decision to reject your ad.

Pentagon Welfare Queens Billboard

The sales rep from AK Media told me our artwork, designed by Stefan Sagmeister, was too offensive to place on a public billboard owned by her esteemed company. No problem, I said, just send us back our $4,500 check with a letter explaining your decision. We had predicted this. Only a billboard company owned by Ralph Nader would accept a billboard depicting the CEOs of America's largest defense contractors dressed in drag as upscale "Welfare Queens." The billboard highlighted the defense industry's habit of taking handouts from the Pentagon—in the form of lucrative contracts for wasteful weapons systems like Star Wars. So, once we got the letter of rejection from the billboard company's sales rep, informing us that our design was too "offensive to the community," we churned out a news release with these headlines: "Billboard Company Rejects 'Pentagon Welfare Queens' Ad for Being 'Offensive to the Community.'" We stated that it's the defense contractors who are offensive to the community. The results? Our ad was actually *printed* in the *Washington Post* and *Boston Globe*, and it generated talk-radio fodder across the country.

The Nose on My Face

Typically, public service announcements are mundane and non-controversial. Greenpeace chose to offer TV stations in Nevada and New Mexico a slick, controversial announcement that it knew would be rejected by most stations. The Greenpeace public service announcement depicts a tense, packed public meeting where a government spokesperson is speaking about plans for a radioactive-waste dump. He asks citizens attending the meeting to trust him. But as he speaks, his nose begins to grow longer and longer like Pinocchio's and to glow a radioactive shade of green. Sure enough, most TV stations rejected the "public service announcement," but local newspapers ran articles about the rejected ad ("Air Time Sought for Anti-Nuclear Spot") and local TV stations' news shows ran the entire ad as part of the news coverage of the controversy.

Deliver or Hand Out Something

Letter-writing campaigns can be effective, but they don't often grab much media attention. But many nonprofit groups have realized that augmenting a letter-writing campaign by delivering *something else* to a politician can make big news, especially if you deliver it when your issue is already in the news. Any object can be delivered.

Pot Giveaway

State law in California—and elsewhere—allows marijuana to be grown and distributed to very sick people, if they have a doctor's prescription for it. Federal law, however, prohibits

This advertisement got national news coverage after a billboard company rejected it for being "offensive to the community."
CREDIT: RUCKUS SOCIETY

this. As a result, agents from the federal Drug Enforcement Agency raided a medical marijuana pot farm in California, confiscating 130 plants, even though the farm was legal in California. In response, members of the Santa Cruz City council staged a high-profile "pot giveaway" in front of City Hall to emphasize their position that, at least in Santa Cruz, using marijuana for medical purposes made sense.

Hangers, Paper Plates, and Shells

Other activists have hand-delivered hangers, illustrating the ramifications of an abortion ban; fortune cookies, with a peace fortune inside; dunce caps; paper plates, showing the plight of the hungry; and the ashes of cremated AIDS victims, highlighting policies related to the treatment of the disease.

March, Dance, Snort— Anything Except a Rally

I'm not a fan of rallies. They're tedious for participants and the media alike—even though it feels good to be in a group of like-minded citizens. But even this is not an excuse for holding a rally—because there are many alternatives (or additions to a rally) that are more fun and interesting for everybody involved. Even a fifteen-minute march tacked on to a rally has a bit more visual appeal than a rally. But you should think even more broadly, drawing on the ideas below and elsewhere in this chapter.

Students March for Three Days

A teacher in a large metropolitan school district led a group of fifty students on a three-day, sixty-mile march to protest cuts in the education budget. As they approached the capitol, carrying signs such as "Your Future Depends on My Education," the high school students were joined by 150 more of their peers. Along the way, their saga—sore ankles, sunburn, and other discomforts—attracted the full flock of local media. A series of stories appeared, starting when they began their march and concluding with their rally at the capitol.

Snort-In Against the War

In the 1960s political activists held sit-ins and teach-ins for civil rights and against the Vietnam war. Freshen up this tactic by executing any kind of "-in." For example, I was able to convince Ben Cohen, co-founder of Ben and Jerry's, to stage a "snort-in" against the Iraq war. With a pig nose firmly attached to his face, Ben declared, "Now is *not* the time for the American people to wallow. We must speak out against the war." Then he led the crowd in a group snort. Later, San Francisco activists tested the maxim that "all news coverage is good news coverage" by staging a "vomit-in" against the Iraq war.

The Long March

If you've got the time, the longer you march, the better as far as the media are concerned. Remember "Granny D," who became a spokeswoman for campaign finance reform as she walked from California to Washington, D.C.? And how about the three men who gained local coverage for moonwalking for three days (for the cause of renewable energy), trying to set a record for the *Guinness Book of World Records*? Activists rode around the country in a van sculpted to look like a Pentagon pig, which generated lots of local coverage.

Other Rally Alternatives

Try run-athoning, dance-athoning, skate-athoning, or any-athoning. As one group of dancing activists did, you can "kick up a protest" simply by joining arms and doing "high kicks" at a rally. Also consider "encircling" a target, as explained below.

Bait the Opposition

Conflict makes news. Aware of this, some activists deliberately confront or bait their opponents into battle, and then draw attention to the tempest.

Picking a Fight on Campus

David Horowitz, a notorious conservative, placed ads in college newspapers denouncing reparations (monetary or otherwise) for African-Americans due to slavery. Instead, the ads stated that black Americans are indebted to the country for their freedom. Some college newspaper editors refused the ad, generating controversy and media attention. Others ran it, and were later forced to apologize. At one campus, students upset over the ad removed bundles of newspapers from newsstands on campus. The furor about political correctness, freedom of speech, civil rights, and much more generated wide coverage, including a front-page piece in the *New York Times*.

Conflict at a Political Event

Some activists manipulate news coverage of a large event by creating a conflict. An organization may draw thousands of people to a rally only to have the media focus on a debate or disturbance among people in a small group. (A photo with "both sides" can appeal to editors.) For example, a small number of antiabortion protesters have attended large pro-choice rallies, creating a confrontation and landing a "pro-and-anti-choice face-off" photo in the newspaper. (If you see this kind of conflict happening at an event you've organized, tell the reporters who may rush to cover it that it does not represent your event at all.)

Create a Spectacle

Journalists have an eye out for the unusual, and sometimes simply creating a spectacle at the right time can generate coverage. I can't tell you when a "spectacle" goes too far, from the media's perspective, to cover. But here are some examples to help you make your own decision.

Flush the Toilets

What's more painful than a ribbon-cutting ceremony to announce the opening of a new building? Not much. There are plenty of other ways to make the point. Here's one: one hundred fifty students of the McDonough Arts Magnet School in Lowell, Massachusetts, showed that the new Tsongas Arena was ready to go by simultaneously flushing all the toilets.

Exorcism of the Pentagon

During the Vietnam War, Abbie Hoffman hatched the idea of surrounding the Pentagon and, as part of a religious ceremony, exorcising its evil. The police refused to let the hippies encircle the Pentagon, and Hoffman didn't have enough people to do it anyway. But the media event proceeded with the hippies chanting into an amplification system (as quoted in Marty Jezer's book *Abbie Hoffman, American Rebel*): "In the name of the generative power of Priapus, in the name of the totality, we call upon the demons of the Pentagon to rid themselves of the cancerous tumors of the war generals." The plan created quite a bit of media hype and to this day is one of the best-known hippie stunts of the 1960s. But according to Jezer's book, it was actually a tiny part of a 50,000-person march on the Lincoln Memorial. (Hoffman was a spectacle master, by his own admission more concerned with visual presentation than factual analysis. He was the one who illustrated the greed of Wall Street by throwing dollar bills from the visitors' gallery of the New York Stock Exchange and watching the traders dive for them. In a lesser-known protest opposing traffic in New York City, he organized a "do-your-own-thing" event, temporarily shutting down St. Marks Place with dancing hippies.)

Burning the Puppy

In his strange book *How You Can Manipulate the Media*, David Alexander describes an incident in which a man announced to the news media that he was going to pour gasoline on a puppy and burn it at a news conference. Newspapers ran stories about his plans, and of course citizens were outraged. The police could do nothing because it was not a crime to threaten to kill a puppy. At the scheduled news conference, a man emerged with a puppy in his arms. With live cameras rolling (it was the 5 P.M. news hour), he criticized journalists for caring more about puppies than people and expressed outrage at U.S. foreign policy in Central America. He said he would not burn the puppy after all.

Kiss a Pig, Throw a Tomato, and Chuck a Pumpkin

A principal generated a mini-media event when he kissed a pot-bellied pig as a payoff for students meeting his challenge to read 140,000 minutes in February. At the annual tomato festival in Bunol, Spain, citizens pelt each other with over 100 tons of ripe tomatoes. And then there's the Morton, Illinois, "Pumpin' Chuckin' Contest," in which contestants launch pumpkins with cannons and other devices. One participant said that his goal is to have the first pumpkin to break the sound barrier.

Encircle a Target

Again, it's worth thinking long and hard before organizing a traditional march or rally. Journalists look at these honorable means of democratic expression as boring. You might ask yourself, how can we involve a large group of people in our "rally" yet not have a rally? One way is to encircle something, perhaps a building, a statue, anything that might be relevant to your issue. You don't even have to use people to encircle your target. Ribbons, tape, or other objects might do the trick.

A Human Chain

Activists in Boulder, Colorado, repeatedly tried to form a human chain around the ten-square-mile Rocky Flats nuclear-bomb plant. Each time they undertook the protest, they received substantial media coverage, though some reporters emphasized their failure to accomplish the encirclement rather than their point that the plant should be closed. Nonetheless, photographs of segments of the encirclement, with people holding hands in front of the fenced, austere bomb plant, were irresistible to TV and print photographers.

Circles of Banned Books

Students listed the titles of banned books on separate pieces of paper and linked them together to form a paper chain used to encircle the library during Banned Books Week.

Burn Something

Fire is a good visual that makes news. Just look at the media events that rage around small forest fires or, for that matter, any fire. You can use fire, too, but you don't necessarily have to break the law or destroy anything significant to do it. You will have to be careful that your activity does not alienate your supporters.

Burning the Budget

Jon Caldera, a conservative foe of an initiative that would have provided child care and other services for kids in Denver, took the not-so-bold step of burning three dollar bills on the steps of the state capitol, symbolizing the $3,000 each Colorado couple would, in his view, have wasted if the amendment passed, which it did not. For the three dollars, he got priceless PR out of the stunt.

Flag-Burning

Notice how often burning the American flag is in the news. It's the stereotyped photo for anti-American demonstrations around the world. Consider if it makes sense to burn a different flag than the stars and stripes. Something like the McDonald's flag?

Present Your Organization in Action

Often, you don't need to stage anything for reporters. Simply let them know when your organization is doing something interesting, particularly if it has visual appeal. Every day, nonprofit groups are doing interesting things, but too frequently staff and volunteers forget about letting the news media know. Depending on how busy journalists are on a given day, almost any community activity—even a meeting—can make news. (Also see Chapter 20, "Suggest Story Ideas to Journalists.")

Police Arrest Suspected Prostitutes

It appeared that the front-page newspaper photo and television news video of a police officer arresting a suspected prostitute was the result of photographers just happening to be in the right place at the right time—or listening to the police radio. But luck had nothing to do with it. Knowing that the opportunity to photograph prostitutes being apprehended by police could be attractive to news outlets, the police department invited journalists to accompany officers on a sting operation, which resulted in thirteen arrests.

Other Newsworthy Organizational Activities

Boy Scouts practice survival skills in a mock disaster. A day-care class goes to the park on "kite day." A church group removes graffiti from underpasses. Salvation Army staffers hand out survival kits to the homeless on a winter morning.

Link Your Event to a Season or Holiday

Reporters are constantly looking for new ways to cover the holidays or seasonal changes. From a journalist's perspective, the holidays *have* to be covered. Yet the same old stuff doesn't grab people. Take advantage of this by offering journalists something different to cover.

"Hell House" Haunted House

Extreme right-wing activists in various cities make national news with a "haunted house" around Halloween. The "horrors" in the house, located at a church, include bloody "abortions," drug-addicted teens, gay marriage, lesbian suicide, and other symbols of the right-wing political agenda. The haunted house is often denounced by pro-choice activists, which propels the story further in the media.

Memorial Day, Valentine's Day, and Prom Night

The surgeon general's recommendations on drunk driving were released around Memorial Day to take advantage of journalists' interest in drunk driving during that weekend. Valentine's Day was used by Planned Parenthood to offer discounts on vasectomies. Groups concerned about teenage drunk driving have used the prom season to inject their concerns in the news. Environmentalists raise awareness on Earth Day by planting trees. Community organizers use the biggest shopping day of the year (the day after Thanksgiving) to draw attention to unsafe toys or "No Shopping Day." Activists have dressed as Scrooge, Santa Claus, or a mad Easter Bunny to make a point on holidays.

Write Simple Reports

Look, if the Purina dog food company can score major media attention for its study of the "Pet-Healthiest Cities," you can write a report that will garner coverage, too. Lengthy reports with credible data frequently make news, but so do easy-to-write reports with anecdotal or subjective information. You can devise a creative "report" that could make news, particularly if it's released when your issue is in the news. (See Chapter 31, "Publicize a Report or Academic Paper.")

Beer or Presidents

The Center for Science in the Public Interest in Washington, D.C., focuses on health issues. It often releases detailed reports analyzing the fat content of foods. In a simple study, however, the organization surveyed just a few fourth-grade classes near Washington. The center asked students to name U.S. presidents and brands of beer. The fourth-graders could not only name more brands of beer than presidents but were more likely to spell the beer brands correctly. These findings received wide coverage—as did a much more expensive and complex academic study revealing that children were as likely to identify Joe Camel (the cartoon figure on Camel cigarettes) as they were Mickey Mouse.

News or "News"

Rocky Mountain Media Watch filed a petition with the Federal Trade Commission, arguing that the "news" presented on local stations was so saturated with mayhem and fluff that it was not, in fact, news. And, therefore, for local stations to advertise their "news" as news constituted false advertising. Unfortunately, the FTC did not agree, but the stunt generated national coverage.

Raise Money for an Alternative

A bake sale isn't news. But if you're having one to raise money to pay off the national deficit, it can be. A self-mocking fund-raiser like this can be newsworthy. When I was a college student, the Brown Disarmament Group opposed decisions by professors to accept Defense Department grants to help devise Star Wars, the space-based missile system. Professors responded to our opposition by claiming that they could not fund their research, which had civilian applications, any other way. To illustrate the predicament, our group staged a bake sale to raise money to replace a Brown professor's Star Wars grant. We hoped that the media coverage of the bake sale might inspire some rich person to dump a pile of money on us. Unfortunately, it didn't, and we raised a total of $63, but we made news and made people think.

Fund-Raise

You can raise money and raise your profile at the same time. And have fun. Here are a few ideas.

Flamingoes

In a cheeky fund-raiser, students placed dozens of pink, plastic flamingoes in the lawns of people they knew. For $10, you could have the flamingoes sent elsewhere. For $25, you could ensure that they never come back.

Paint Piggy Banks

The Brownies Troop 1588 painted piggy banks, which were "adopted" by businesses and donors. The money raised was given to a nonprofit providing services for children.

Dogwash

The Deer Creek Animal Hospital grabbed headlines when it staged an outdoor dogwash. Dog washers scrubbed down the hounds as part of a benefit.

More Fund-Raising Ideas

Nonprofits have auctioned hand-painted masks and flip-flops. (But do this during the day, when more reporters are available.) If your town doesn't have a running race with pets involved, like the "furry scurry," start one.

Craft a Puppet

Puppet-making is one of the most beautiful activist art forms. Large puppets add visual intensity to any event, and are a smart way to emphasize a message.

FrankenCorn and FrankenSalmon

Activists concerned about genetically modified foods use puppets, like FrankenCorn, to simplify their point. They carry their puppets in front of hearings, meetings, or political events.

Political Puppets

Often using papier-mâché, activists sculpt the heads of political leaders, presenting them on sticks as ghoulish figures—or simply wearing their heads.

Healthy Teeth, Healthy Kids

A puppet does not have to be a human figure at all. Use the same techniques to make signs that will stand out at an otherwise ho-hum rally. At a rally for funding for more dental care for kids, children held up a giant toothbrush emblazoned with the message "Healthy Teeth, Healthy Kids."

Sponsor an Art Show

The idea of activism being "art" is not new. Abbie Hoffman, the yippie media manipulator, described his media antics this way: "We would hurl ourselves across the canvas of society like streaks of splattered paint." By addressing social issues or public policy, artists often make their work newsworthy.

Art on a Stick

When I worked for Greenpeace, a University of Colorado graduate student named Craig Freeman approached us with the idea of placing his art on twelve billboards that were sitting empty at the gates of Rocky Flats, a nuclear-bomb plant. He knew that

Greenpeace was concerned about Rocky Flats, and in fact we had been inquiring about renting the billboards. We ended up forming a partnership in which we used his images and our words on six of the billboards and he retained complete control of the remaining six billboards for his work, which also related to Rocky Flats. It was a good deal for him because Greenpeace paid for all his materials and publicized the project, generating national media attention. (In an amusing twist that spawned interest by news media, another activist group protested Greenpeace's use of the billboards—even though they were at the gates of the nuclear-bomb factory—because billboards them-selves are an environmental blight, or as one of the anti-Greenpeace activists put it, "Billboards are litter on a stick.")

Also consider these media-genic tactics:

- Painting a mural (Contact reporters when it's being painted.)
- Bird-dogging (Create a character that dogs a politician or shows up repeatedly at events.)
- Celebrating
- Rallying for what you *don't* want (mutants for nuclear power)
- Altering or co-opting your opponent's symbol or sign (See Chapter 41, "Spray, Stick, Cover . . .")
- Marking an anniversary (Pay attention to the one-year anniversaries of major events.)
- Assembling a group of unusual suspects (rich people against the estate tax)
- Offering a reward (a billboard offering a reward for crime information)
- Borrowing a sports team's mascot or creating your own
- Fasting
- Boycotting (Don't patronize Taco Bell) or girlcotting (Buy nuclear-free New Zealand lamb!)
- Pledging to do something (Kids pledge not to smoke. Children ask politicians to pledge not to close their school.)
- Connecting your issue to entertainment programming (If your issue will be fictionalized on *West Wing*, before the show airs tell reporters *at the TV station that carries the show* about what you are doing locally.)

- Singing (Ben of Ben and Jerry's is great to work for because he'll take any PR idea seriously, no matter how wacky. So when I presented him with a rap song written by me and my wife, it did not surprise me that he was up for singing it— which he did on national TV and elsewhere.)

FOOLISH *AND* CREDIBLE

When I hold media workshops, I often show images of activists dressing as pigs, delivering coffins, dropping banners from buildings, and more. I explain that I started my career wearing a giant Mr. Taco costume and endured kids yanking on my lettuce and cheese. I emphasize the importance of creating engaging events and campaigns.

Often, people listen to my advice and tell me that my approach is not for them. Yes, they say, it's OK to take risks, act silly, or be confrontational if you work for Greenpeace or some other marginalized group, but we are trying to reach a mainstream audience. So we are going to stick with news conferences featuring well-dressed snore inducers.

This unfortunate thinking keeps cause-oriented groups on the sidelines of society.

Politicians, like President George W. Bush, do silly things to get media attention—like "pardoning" a turkey prior to Thanksgiving— without damaging their "credibility." So can you.
CREDIT: AP/WIDE WORLD PHOTOS

Communicating with humor, confrontation, and stunts is everyday fare for corporations, politicians, or anyone who's serious about getting media attention. Politics has been reduced largely to a clash of symbols and symbolic actions that are media-friendly.

Mainstream politicians are as enamored with stunts as anyone. There are many examples; let's start with the president and work down. George W. Bush didn't think it would hurt his credibility to share a news conference with a turkey, literally. As smarter presidents did before him, Bush "pardoned" a turkey prior to Thanksgiving.

To focus the media spotlight on Sen. Bob Dole's ties to tobacco companies, a Democratic Party activist dressed as Buttman and showed up at Dole events. CREDIT: MIKE ALTSCHULE

Also consider that one of the lasting images of President Clinton's campaign against Sen. Bob Dole was the Democratic National Committee's use of "Buttman," a party activist dressed in a cigarette-butt costume. Buttman dogged Dole around the country, linking him to the tobacco companies.

Then, how about this: The reelection campaign of Gov. Roy Romer of Colorado sent a "duck" to the rallies of his opponent to drive home Romer's point that his opponent was "ducking" his challenge to debate. In a survey of election coverage of the governor's race, the duck stunt ran away with more air time on TV than coverage of most other election topics. This came shortly before Sen. Ben Nighthorse Campbell, Republican of Colorado, raffled off the opportunity to cut off his trademark ponytail.

The point is that "serious" and "credible" communication is not limited to news conferences featuring well-dressed people standing behind podiums. Images and symbols—both sophomoric and aggressive—communicate to everyone, and should be used by anyone who wants to communicate effectively. Find the right people in your group to execute stunts, and get to work. (See Chapter 9, "Brainstorm Stunt Ideas.")

Part TWO

Landing on *Oprah* Is Not a Strategy

Some activists believe that if they catch the attention of Oprah, they win. They think media coverage is an end in itself. It isn't. Efforts to land in the news should be connected to a *strategy* for achieving a political victory or solving a social problem.

All the media attention in the world—including all the stunts discussed in Part One—are of limited use unless they are part of a communications plan.

This section outlines the basics of how to set up a strategic media program and how to interact effectively with journalists *over the long haul*. This will allow you to be successful not only at getting news coverage but also at actually changing something in the real world.

2

What's Newsworthy?

Your ultimate goal as a publicist is to be able to think like a journalist. To do this, you have to understand what's newsworthy—what journalists want. That's why this chapter is essential reading, a prerequisite to everything else in this book.

You need to be clear about this first: There is no definition of "news." In his classic book *Reporters and Officials*, Leon V. Sigal writes that news is what's in the news. This is the best nondefinition that I've found. It means that the only way to understand what's news is to consume great quantities of it yourself.

The definition of news is just as murky for journalists, who decide what's news every day. For example, one young TV news reporter told an activist friend of mine that she was confused about how "news" was defined at her TV station in Los Angeles. Whenever she asked her boss if a particular story was newsworthy, he would ask her, "Does it wiggle?" What does this mean? Who knows.

I asked some of the journalists what "newsworthy" meant to them:

"What's newsworthy?" asks Keith Rogers, a reporter for the *Las Vegas Review Journal* in Nevada. "You have to look at your audience. We're touching people's lives who read the newspaper."

"Every news day is different," says Cathy McFeaters, news director for KVUE-TV in Austin, Texas, an ABC affiliate. "And every situation is different. That's the thing about news. I always get nervous when I hear simple definitions of what news is."

"If it's Sunday and nothing is happening, anything can be news," says Krystian Orlinski, a Los Angeles–based editor for Reuters Television, a news service.

"The sexy and trendy and interesting stuff will take precedence over the long-range stuff," says *Denver Post* reporter Jack Cox. "That's how news decisions are made."

In the end, defining "newsworthy" is more of an intuitive process than a rational one. The more news you consume, the easier it will be for you to understand what's news to different news outlets.

Here's an example of the television journalist's mind at work: Tom Marshall, a staffer for the Rocky Mountain Peace and Justice Center, was once trying to persuade a CBS News producer to do a story on the transport of nuclear waste from Denver to southern New Mexico. The producer listened to Tom and said she wanted to show the possible impacts on children. "Is there a school on the route?" she asked.

Characteristics of News

There are a number of characteristics commonly associated with a "news" story. The more of these characteristics connected with your news story, the more coverage it will likely get:

- Novelty
- Shock
- Conflict
- New data
- Simplicity
- Kids
- Social issues or a prominent public figure involved
- Humor
- Outdoor location
- Action
- Bright props and images
- News stories about the event published in advance
- Local impact

Following are some characteristics of an event that will keep many journalists away:

- Indoor location
- People reading scripts
- A private, profit-oriented goal
- Complexity
- Unknown participants
- Bad timing or remote location

A story with credible, new data about a timely subject is often of most interest to a print reporter and not necessarily of interest to a television reporter, who needs visual imagery. If you've got new information and a visual to go along with it, you've got the strongest story for the widest variety of journalists.

However, even stories *without* "hard" data are widely covered by all kinds of media. Image-based or ironic stories can be just as newsworthy as a 250-page report full of new statistics.

For activists, it's critical to take advantage of "news hooks" to get coverage. This means that you hook your story to something that's already in the news. For example, if a woman is killed by a drunk driver and you run a program educating teens about the dangers of drunk driving, tell the news media about it when a related story is in the news. (See Chapter 21, "Hook Your Story to Breaking News.")

Images for Television

From parenting to politics, television is clearly the most dominant force in American life. If you want to communicate with most Americans, you have to use images and symbols that can be beamed through the tube. (See Chapter 1, "Think Outside the Stratosphere.")

"The question is not what you want to say, but what you will be able to *show*," says Claus Kleber, a Washington, D.C., correspondent for KRD, German public television. "Come up with something visual."

"A meeting, I don't care about," says Deborah Clayton, an assignment editor for KVBC-TV, the NBC affiliate in Las Vegas. "Television needs to be visually stimulating."

"If it doesn't have good pictures, people won't put it on the air," says Peter Dykstra, a senior producer for Cable News Network in Atlanta.

Eat Bread, Water, and the News

Most activists like to read the newspaper and hide out on the soothing planet of National Public Radio, and yet they think they know what's newsworthy. Negative.

The only way to understand the news is to absorb as much of it as you can stomach, even from the sources activists love to hate, like local TV news and conservative talk radio. You should take in everything, everywhere you see it. In the coffee shop. On the Web. In the TV section of Target, if you must go there. Don't be a selective news junkie.

You have to know what "news" is being dished out to the public. Then you can match what you're publicizing with media that might bite. More important, you will be able to develop a sense for what's news for various media outlets and develop events and stories accordingly.

3

Strategic Media Plans

Entire lifetimes are spent studying communications theory and practice. A library of books has been written on these topics. And plenty of people get multiple academic degrees in related disciplines. So it's not surprising that you may be intimidated by the idea of developing a strategic communications plan.

In reality, however, for the working stiff who's trying to communicate basic ideas to everyday people, it simply isn't that hard. You just need to write a brief planning document answering the following common-sense questions: What's your goal? Who's your audience? What's your message? And which news outlets will "move your message" to your target audience? Once these questions are answered, you should develop a work plan, including a timeline, to try to score coverage from targeted media outlets.

What's Your Goal?

Before leaping into a media campaign, assure yourself that a media campaign makes sense. Manipulating the media is a tool, one tool among many, that an activist can use to make a difference. After you study an issue, it may turn out that instead of focusing scarce energy or dollars on trying to get media attention, it's a better idea to expend your resources elsewhere—say, to hire a lawyer.

Many different goals can justify a media campaign. You may want to raise more money, find more volunteers, affect politics—

or simply increase your organization's name recognition. Make sure your goal is clear and get on with it.

Who's Your Audience(s)?

If your goal is to affect politics, whose mind do you need to change to win? Does the mayor have the ultimate power? Perhaps the buck stops at the city council or the air-quality commission or the school board?

Once you've identified key decisionmakers, figure out who can influence them. Whom do you need to activate or convince? What group of people could sway your decisionmakers?

Usually the answer to these questions is not the general public but instead a segment of the general public. For example, if you are trying to affect the vote of a specific state legislator, you will probably need to reach residents of the legislator's district, a defined *geographic* area. Or you may target a specific age group, like elderly voters, within a geographic area. Or you may target swing voters, like soccer moms, who represent a specific *demographic* group, based on age, income, geographic, and other information. Some people target a psychographic, a group of people with shared values and beliefs.

Your target audience could turn out to be just a handful of people, like the board of directors of a corporation or of a key foundation. Or perhaps just one person, like the husband or wife of a key member of the board of directors.

What's Your Message and Who Are Your Spokespeople?

Next, you need to figure out the words, images, and phrases that will communicate most effectively to your target audience. Also think about which spokespeople your audience will believe. Some organizations, like Mothers Against Drunk Driving, use victims as spokespeople. Others use celebrities, politicians, or people of stature, like retired generals or experts.

Activists often make the *unforgivable* mistake of *assuming* that they know what their target audiences will understand and like. Never trust your own judgment. Test your ideas on your target audience first. There are three ways to do this: polls, focus groups, and the brother-in-law test.

Polls

Think of a poll as way to answer these questions and more: Does your target audience support your position? What argument does it support most strongly? Least strongly? Who are the right spokespeople? What images, phrases, and words appeal most to your target audience? Where does your target audience get its news? A poll is a comprehensive tool to gauge public sentiment. (See "Examples of Different Ways to Frame a Political Debate" below.)

Use polling data to help you figure out what your organizational goals should be. For example, because polling data showed that there is not much support in the United States for fewer prisons or the rehabilitation of prisoners instead of incarceration, a group of activists calling for prison reform decided they would first focus their message on the evils of solitary confinement and move on to other prison issues later.

Most politicians use polling data extensively. They develop images, political positions, and sound bites based on public opinion data. For example, you may have heard the joke that President Clinton didn't go to the bathroom without taking a poll first. The truth behind the joke is that Clinton seldom made any political move without consulting polling data first. And President George W. Bush is no different.

A typical poll costs tens of thousands of dollars, but there are cheaper ways to access useful polling data. On a variety of Websites, you can type in key words relating to your issue and look at poll results on point. (See "Public Opinion Research" in Part Eight of "Resources.")

Focus Groups

A focus group is a meeting of a sample of your target audience, maybe six to twelve people assembled to review and discuss any aspect of your campaign—from phrases and spokespeople to flyers and TV advertisements. A moderator asks carefully prepared questions of the group, stops anyone from dominating, and tries to elicit unbiased views. Usually a series of meetings of focus groups composed of different samples of your target audience are held, because one such meeting can more easily provide skewed data.

Costing about $5,000 and up, focus group evaluations are cheaper than polls, and they are intended to obtain much of the same opinion data, but they aren't scientific. They are more accurate and useful if conducted by professionals who will provide you with a written report, but you can conduct them yourself as well.

Brother-in-Law Test

Most of us don't have the time or money to conduct polls or focus groups. But we know we should find some way to test words, spokespeople, phrases, or images on an audience before using them in our communications work. In his book *Spin Works*, Robert Bray offers the most practical way for activists to do this: Find one person who represents your target audience, and meet with him or her—or call him or her up on the phone. Bray recommends finding a family member—he uses his brother-in-law, who he says is a decent suburban fellow—but anyone will do, as long as he or she matches the profile of your target audience.

No matter which technique you use—polls, focus groups, or your brother-in-law—the benefits of conducting opinion research could make the difference between success and failure.

Politics is a battle over words and symbols. This has always been the case, but it's even more true now as fewer people bother to become informed about political issues. So, the words and symbols that you use to argue or "frame" your story and issue can make the difference between victory and defeat.

Examples of Different Ways to "Frame" a Political Debate

- **Abortion.** Those who favor criminalizing abortion want to frame the issue around the question of "Is abortion murder?" because polls show that a large segment of the public believes that abortion is murder. Pro-choice activists want the abortion debate focused on "Who decides?" because polls also show that most people believe it's a woman's choice. Pro-choice activists first started to win the abortion debate after determining—through polling—that the public responded much more favorably to the "choice" argument than to the position that abortion is *not* murder.

- **Affordable Housing.** Under one frame, activists make the argument that the "working poor" need temporary "government assistance" as they move toward complete self-sufficiency. Opponents argue that government "handouts" don't do anything for the "lazy." Polls show that Americans are not persuaded by the argument that they have a moral responsibility to help the poor, but they are willing to help poor people help themselves.
- **Estate Tax Versus Death Tax.** Voters are much more supportive of an "estate" tax than a "death" tax, even though both terms refer to the same thing: a federal tax on the estates of the wealthiest citizens. Once the public debate was switched from abolishing the estate tax to abolishing the death tax, the proposal gained popularity and eventually became law.
- **Teenager Versus Adolescent.** The general public responds much more favorably to the word "adolescent," which people see as a kid in a difficult period in life, than to the word "teenager," which they see as a dangerous criminal. So, those trying to gain support for "teen services" would be better off using the word "adolescent."
- **Military Versus Pentagon.** For most people, the word "military" conjures up positive images of our soldiers. The word "Pentagon," in contrast, is associated with negative images of defense contractors and bureaucratic waste. Those arguing for Pentagon budget cuts would want to avoid the word "military."

Which Media Outlets
Reach Your Target Audience?

Once you've decided what you want to say to whom, you should figure out which news sources are consumed by your target audiences. For example, politicians and policymakers read the op-ed and letters pages of the newspaper carefully. Foundation types read the *Chronicle of Philanthropy*. If you are trying to reach teenagers, don't aim to get coverage by local TV news—because few watch it. Similarly, talk radio shows often draw more conservative, male audiences. So, duh, don't go for talk radio if you are trying to reach young, liberal women. Or, if you do, make sure you target the right talk show.

The data you collect from polling or focus groups—even if it's a focus group of one—should help you figure out where your target audience gets its news. You can also pretend you are a potential advertiser and ask the advertising departments of news outlets for a "rate sheet," which will describe the audience of the news outlet's shows.

Then you need to select and execute media activities that will be covered by your target audience's favorite news sources. That's what Parts Three and Four of this book will help you do.

Write Your Plan

There's no standard time period that a media plan should cover. Your organization may develop multiple plans for various projects. A media plan can focus on, say, the three months leading up to a single event (for example, a human encirclement of your senator's office) or on a multi-year campaign (such as the promotion of a specific bill in the state legislature) or anything in between. I usually recommend that an organization has, at a minimum, a one-year plan that is updated annually and covers varied media activities during the year.

You should have a document with written goals, audiences, messages, and media outreach activities linked to a calendar. You should set achievable and measurable media goals (such as ten letters-to-the-editor, two op-eds, one media event, one news briefing). Your plan might also include media training for staff, board members, or volunteers.

Ideally, your *media plan* should be a component of a broader *communications plan*, covering a longer time period, perhaps five years. This document should address not only the news media but all aspects of your organization's public profile (speeches, flyers, posters, paid advertising, events, business cards, newsletters, alerts, fund-raising appeals, annual reports, and so on). The best communications plans include a long-term vision about how you want to shape public opinion about your issue *and* organization.

4

Starting Your
Media Program

You need to overcome mental and organizational barriers before getting your media program under way. This chapter will help you do this.

First, convince yourself and your colleagues that media coverage of your cause will help your organization.

Benefits of Media Coverage

- A better chance of winning. You can achieve little or nothing in public life without a sterling communications plan. Whether it's winning an election ("It's the economy, stupid."), passing a law, or changing public opinion, communication is central.
- Increased funding. Like other people, funders are impressed with an organization that gets media attention. It adds authority and credibility to your programs.
- Higher morale. Whether they are volunteering, answering the phones, or typing the newsletter, people feel better about their work when they are recognized for it. It feels good when friends approach you in the supermarket and congratulate you or thank you for something you are doing at the office.
- More volunteers. Even the smallest media hit can bring volunteers to your doorstep. After landing an article in a neighborhood paper, an organization promoting environmental projects by teachers was flooded with volunteers.

- Responsibility to the wider community. People should know about their communities—especially about social ills and people trying to fix them. Your fellow citizens need to know about the homeless, the hungry, the angry, the disenfranchised. If our social problems remain out of sight, they can be conveniently ignored by our leaders.
- Unknown good stuff. It's a big world out there, and by connecting to it through the news media, you make things happen. You're in the paper and you get a call from a citizen who has been trying to do something about the same problem for years and turns out to be a great ally. Someone reads about your efforts and secretly leaks you vital information. Someone drops a $5,000 check in your mailbox. It's all happened to me.

The most common arguments against doing more media outreach—and responses to them—are:

- The media will distort our views. Yes, the news media have unfairly destroyed careers and organizations. But you will lower the likelihood of this substantially by refining your message, dealing effectively with reporters, and initiating a media campaign involving fewer risks. (However, if the news media do consistently distort your views, document it, and confront them with the information. See www.fair.org.)
- It won't get done. Media work at nonprofits is often pushed to the back burner by managers—and then deemed a failure. Staff have to be given time to work on it, and blocks of time for it should be set aside. Provide adequate resources.
- The media don't care about our issue. Unlikely. Brush up on your media and communications skills before making this assessment. Then decide which elements of a communications program will work.

Basic Tools for Effective Media Work

- Don't assume you know what you are doing. Take a media training class and read a few guidebooks in addition to this one.

- You need a basic office setup with good computer and software (Internet access, phone, stationery, VCR, television).
- Find access to appropriate media lists (See "Lists of News Outlets and Journalists" in Part Eight, "Resources.")
- Keep up-to-date on trends in journalism and public relations by ordering subscriptions to a few publications covering the journalism and PR worlds: *Adbusters, American Journalism Review, Columbia Journalism Review, PR Watch,* and *PR Week.*
- Sign up for list-serves that distribute news articles about communications. One excellent source is the Benton Foundation's (www.benton.org) "Communications-Related Headlines" daily news service.
- Read a few of the following books: *Strategic Communications for Nonprofits* by Kathy Bonk et al., *Spin Works* by Robert Bray, *Breaking the News* by James Fallows, *Guerrilla PR* by Michael Levine, *How to Watch TV News* by Neil Postman and Steve Powers, and *News for a Change: An Advocate's Guide to Working with the Media* by Lawrence Wallack, Katie Woodruff, Lori Dorfman, and Iris Diaz.
- Stay current on the news by consuming as many national and local news sources as possible.
- Assemble a basic media kit for your organization. (See Chapter 18, "News Conferences and Media Kits.")

Working with Media Consultants

As you move forward, you may consider hiring a media consultant for media training or other services, such as media relations (to generate news coverage), logo design, message development, advertising (to develop and place ads), event planning, publication design (to produce newsletters, reports, and so on), direct mail, conference planning, photodocumentation, speech writing, and Web development.

If you hire a consultant, make sure your needs match his or her strengths. You can hire a big company or a sole operator. Be clear about what's expected, shop for prices, and get references, including samples of previous work, if appropriate.

5

Cultivate Relationships with Journalists

O<small>N RARE OCCASIONS, YOU WILL</small> stage a single media event and your cause will be won. For example, authorities at a New York mall recently asked a woman who was breastfeeding her newborn to leave. The woman fought back, organizing a dozen women and their babies to breastfeed in unison in the heart of the mall. In the wake of intense media coverage, including national Associated Press photos of the breastfeeders, the New York legislature gave women the explicit right to breastfeed in malls and elsewhere.

This story of inspired—and successful—activism is not the norm. Usually, victory comes after years of work, taking so long that you may not recognize your "victory" when it arrives. As a result, it's essential to develop relationships with journalists that will endure for the long term.

This chapter contains tips on how to establish ongoing relationships with reporters. This is an extremely important aspect of publicizing a cause. You should continually scrutinize how you interact with journalists and strive to improve, sharpening your public relations skills.

"A lot of what gets covered depends on personal relationships at the paper," acknowledges Colin Covert, a feature reporter for the *Star Tribune* in Minneapolis.

So, you're thinking, what good does that information do me if I have no such contacts? First, recognize that although helpful, contacts aren't essential. Many journalists will listen to you even if they don't know you.

Second, it should inspire you to develop as many contacts as you can. Say you've just started a new job in a new town, and you want to get to know some journalists. What should you do?

"Lunch is too time-consuming," says Jack Broom, a reporter for the *Seattle Times*. "Start with a phone call. Say something like, 'We'd like you to know about us. We've got some events coming up in the next few months. Whom should we contact?'" Starting from there, take advantage of every opportunity to present yourself as a credible source of information for journalists.

Tips on Becoming a Resource for Journalists

- Be available. Give reporters, especially at news services where they work odd hours, your cell and home phone numbers and tell them it's OK to call.
- Seek out journalists at meetings, hearings, and other events and give them your business card.
- Be ready to be quoted. If a reporter calls for a quote about breaking news and you have to call back before you can comment, either because you don't know the answer to a question or need permission to be quoted, you decrease the odds that the reporter will call again. Next time he or she may call someone who does not require the hassle of two phone calls. In fact, you may not be quoted at all because you may not be able to get through to the reporter before deadline. Or he or she may find someone else to comment and file the story before you call back.
- Know your issue. Journalists, even those who focus on one issue area, are usually not specialists. They are generalists who get their information from "sources." Your goal should be to become a source. Read and comment intelligently on developments relating to your cause.
- Don't always assume journalists have received information that you have. Call or e-mail them and ask if they've heard about the upcoming visit of so-and-so or have seen the news release from the government agency or other body.

- Avoid a flood of rhetoric. Most journalists have heard ideo-
logical arguments many times.
- Know your facts. Never offer information unless you are
sure it's true. You can pass on gossip if you label it as such
and are prepared to take responsibility for talking about it.
- Know where to find information fast. A reporter will call
again if you earn a reputation for locating information for
him or her or for suggesting another credible person to call.
But don't promise to find information unless you are sure
you can get it. (Don't necessarily push to be quoted if you
find information for a journalist.)

Tips on Developing Credibility

- Always be accurate. Journalists turn to credible sources for
accurate information. The worst move you can make is to
embarrass a reporter by feeding him or her wrong information. With accuracy as a baseline, you can earn a reputation
as a credible source.
- Be quoted by various outlets. Journalists look at the work
of their peers, and if you're in a story they see, you establish
credibility. That's one reason to make the effort to be
quoted in any outlet.
- Offer information even if you don't expect to be quoted. "If
the only time I hear from you is when you're pitching your
organization, that's of limited value," says Colin Covert, a
feature reporter for the *Star Tribune* in Minneapolis.
- Compliment your adversaries. A journalist is trying to understand a debate. If you show him or her that you can
understand different sides (though your side is right), you
will earn credibility. "Activists tend to present the other
side as nothing more than a pack of lies," says Paul Vam-
vas, a Washington, D.C.–based producer for Worldnet Television. "You should be able to argue the other side, and do
it credibly."
- Don't exaggerate. It's important to present your point of
view in dramatic terms, but don't overdo it.
- Keep track of revolving journalists, who change jobs frequently. For example, some of the reporters interviewed for

this book switched jobs or quit as it was being written. Even if they stay at one publication, they often shift beats (issue areas). Getting the name and title of a journalist right will reflect well on you as a source of information.

Tips on Cultivating a Lasting Relationship with a Journalist

- Different outlets have different deadlines. Learn them so that you don't annoy journalists near their crunch time. Generally, mornings are best for calling journalists, early in the week if possible.
- Don't bother reporters. Most busy reporters don't want you to "check in" for no reason. Call when you have something to say.
- Make life easy for reporters. Have visual images for television and appropriate information for the print media.
- If a reporter calls you for a comment on a story, don't disclose the story to other journalists. A reporter will not be happy about losing an exclusive thanks to you.
- Refrain from thanking a journalist. It's appropriate—on rare occasions—to compliment a journalist for writing a fair and accurate piece, but hold the thank-yous because reporters, as professionals, are not aiming to please you. (You will find columnists or reporters who openly advocate your position. A thank-you call may be appropriate for them, but be wary.)
- Don't assume a journalist is your friend or your enemy. Even if a reporter writes articles sympathetic to your issue, don't assume he or she supports you or your cause. Continue to treat a reporter as a judge or observer until you have good reason to assume otherwise. Of course, it's not uncommon for journalists to become friends with their sources.
- Recognize that journalists aren't independent operators. Sometimes, editors nix their ideas for stories. "Even when someone has me completely convinced, they're only half-way home," says Peter Dykstra, a senior producer for CNN in Atlanta.
- If you see a journalist in a public place or social gathering, approach him or her without being rude. Be friendly.

6

How and When to Complain About Coverage

GOOD REPORTERS ASK GOOD QUESTIONS, and sometimes their best questions seem offensive or irrelevant. But you seldom gain anything by getting angry at a reporter. You win by answering questions *and* staying "on message."

Just as reporters must ask tough questions, it's also a reporter's job to leave you out of the news if he or she deems it appropriate to do so. Reporters are paid to weigh your news against other news. Nevertheless, it's hard not to be annoyed or angry when a reporter misquotes you, writes an inaccurate story, shuts you out of the news, or offends you in some other serious way.

Despite their best efforts to be accurate, journalists make errors. These errors occur in news stories, editorials, columns, features, even in the food section. In his farewell column to *Denver Post* readers, food writer John Kessler wrote, "You've kept me honest through numerous gaffes. You let me know when my Chinese Orange Chicken recipe was missing a key ingredient (chicken)."

With deadline pressures, reduced staffs, information overload, and other complications, it's a wonder mistakes in the news aren't more common. (For a discussion of other common limitations of news reporting, see the "headaches" listed in Chapter 31, "Publicize a Report or Academic Paper.") This means that you should expect mistakes to appear in stories that affect you and your issue. In general, keep the big picture in mind and don't get too worked up about any single error.

Tips for Complaining
About Errors in Stories

- When it comes to complaining, proceed slowly. Remember, a news story is old news tomorrow and usually, by itself, insignificant in the big picture. Bothering a busy reporter about debatable "mistakes" will hurt your cause more than help it. Often, an error is a matter of interpretation. As *Rocky Mountain News* reporter Bill Scanlon put it, "Usually the mistake falls somewhere between my being totally blameless and something that requires a correction."

- If reporters have made significant factual errors in a piece, call them and discuss it. There's a good chance they will be glad you called and will probably not make the mistake next time. Make sure you have credible documentation of your position ready to e-mail.

- If you don't contact a reporter, the error may be repeated. Reporters check their own news outlet's old stories for background information on a new story. Don't let serious errors get institutionalized.

- Don't necessarily demand that a correction be published or aired during the broadcast. Only rarely is an error serious enough to demand a correction for the record.

- If a mistake is made repeatedly, further action on your part could be warranted. If the error is serious enough and if "the reporter's a jerk," says Janet Day, a former business editor for the *Denver Post*, "call the editor." (Call the news director at TV or radio stations.)

- If your organization's activities are repeatedly shut out, call the reporter who covers your issue area and ask why. If the answer is not satisfactory and the problem is ongoing, meet with his or her superiors. But do not expect coverage every time.

- Some activists forget that the newsroom is composed of individuals. Harassing these individuals as if they were a faceless institution will set you and your cause back.

- Consider calling the "readers' representative" or the ombudsman. If you have a problem with a specific newspaper story, you should generally deal directly with the journalist involved. But if you get nowhere, or the disagreement is over a policy set by editors, the ombudsman may be able to help you.

- Don't complain to reporters about headlines. Reporters don't write headlines, and it's often headlines that are inaccurate or misleading. You can complain to editors about headlines, but such complaints usually aren't worth the trouble.
- Don't complain to reporters about spelling, grammar, or printing problems. Again, this is the responsibility of the editors and is better left for retired librarians to worry about.
- Don't complain about a reporter who shows up late to your event, quotes citizens who know nothing about the issue, leaves out information about how people can contact you or how they can attend a meeting, or chooses an unflattering quote. None of these "errors," especially if they are not part of a documentable pattern, merit your complaints. Reporters are people with strengths and faults. Sometimes, I find myself expecting too much of them, maybe because I think their job is so important. But then I remind myself that they are regular working people, sometimes enjoying their jobs, sometimes not.

You can gain some insight into the life of journalists if you watch them when they are not swarming around a press conference or sitting across from you at an interview. If there is a media frenzy in your area, take an hour and observe the journalists during "downtime," when they're waiting for a news conference, eating lunch, or hanging around the entrance to the courthouse.

You'll see ordinary people—not a bunch of mini–Ted Koppels. Most of them are struggling to figure things out just like everybody else.

Here's an anecdote to illustrate: I once organized a rally to oppose the "media frenzy" around the murder of a child named Jon-Benét Ramsey in Boulder, Colorado. The national media had been covering the Ramsey murder in force. About twenty journalists showed up for the rally. For the most part, they covered the rally accurately and with sensitivity. (Many journalists were as sick of covering the story as our group was of reading about it.) As we were packing up our signs to leave, one photographer with a huge camera asked if she could have one of our signs, which depicted a red-eyed black vulture with the word "TeleVulture" beneath it. I said, "Sure, please, have it," and I gave it to her. As I was leaving, I saw her holding the TeleVulture sign above her head as another photographer took her photograph. You could look at this photographer as another thoughtless journalist who thinks it's funny to be called a televulture (it is, actually). But I think it's more accurate to think of her this way: She's a person trying to make the best out of a difficult job—often with low pay and lousy hours—and trying to find humor and enjoyment in it.

Part THREE

How to Stage a Media Event

MEDIA EVENTS ARE THE SOURCE of much of the "news," particularly political news, that lands on the doorstep or spills out of the TV. If you see the president on TV, you're probably looking at coverage of a media event planned and staged by the president's staff. They know that images and symbols on TV overpower words (and, often, deeds) as a vehicle of communication to mass audiences.

You don't need to have a multimillion-dollar budget to pull off a winning media event. All you have to do is understand basic information about how the news media work and know what resources you have (staff, volunteers, cash, props). Then you need to translate information about your cause into a language and form that is easy for the media to report to their audiences.

If you appreciate street theater, drama, and homespun art—like I do—you'll like executing media events. Organizing one is much like directing a play with props and dialogue.

Similarly, if you like to poke fun at people, you'll likely stage effective media events; teasing requires the same natural inclination toward conflict and fun that an activist uses when designing a media stunt.

Staging an event to project your message is essential. Here's why: The news media, particularly television, rarely cover isolated opinions, ideas, or abstract views. Ideas, in the simple and image-dominated language of the media, are generally considered boring (and hence not newsworthy). But with creativity, you can transform an idea or an opinion about a cause into an event that lends itself to media coverage.

7

First, What's
Strategic and Doable?

Before you plunge into organizing a media event, think about what you want to accomplish beyond simply getting in the news. Be clear about your goal, audience, message, and target media outlets. Then think about what you can realistically pull off.

Enough Money, People, Time?

The most common stumbling blocks to organizing a successful media event are money, people, and time. Different kinds of events require different amounts of each. Choose an event that matches your resources.

Bankrolling an expensive event yourself can be a disaster, leaving you burned out and disillusioned. Think carefully about all the expenses associated with your media event from beginning to end and have a realistic plan for raising the money. Costs can add up quickly. Consider, among other possible expenses, printing, insurance, supplies, phone calls, and transportation.

Make sure you can count on the people you think you can count on. If you select an event that requires 100 people, make sure you've got that much support. (It's far better if 150 people show up at a meeting venue that seats 100 than if 150 people partially fill a cavernous hall designed for 500 people.)

Sometimes it's worth taking a risk and organizing a media event that may "fail" for whatever reasons (such as no people, lack of funds, no coverage, bad weather). But it's easy enough to generate coverage with events that are less likely to fail. If, for example, you tell the media you can rally enough people to encircle a toxic plant and you fail, the headline in the next day's paper will look like this, as it did in the *Denver Post*, "Protesters Settle for Broken Circle; 4,200 Turnout for Rally Falls Short." The lead paragraph read: "An estimated 4,200 antinuclear demonstrators, trying to stretch the human chain with bedspreads, banners and even long-stemmed flowers, watched in disappointment yesterday as a planned encirclement of Rocky Flats fizzled into a broken line of protest."

This "negative" coverage can create the impression that your cause lacks support, which in this case was particularly irritating because a turnout of 4,200 people for a political event is excellent. Negative coverage can also cause volunteers to drop out or cause potential volunteers to seek groups that appear more successful.

However, if you are too worried about failing, you may miss a chance for big success. Big risks—expecting 20,000 to turn out for a rally—can have big payoffs. For example, the Million Mom March had fewer than a million people, but that didn't diminish its media coverage. Also consider that a creative, low-budget, "small time" event can generate more coverage than an expensive, complicated event that may fail.

Will the Event Be Fun?

It's a great idea to decide against organizing an event that won't be any fun. Who wants to confirm the stereotype of an angry, bored, foaming-at-the-mouth, and unhappy community organizer? Remember that author and anarchist Emma Goldman said that if she couldn't dance, she didn't want to be in the revolution.

8

As Thoreau
Said: Simplify

IDENTIFY ONE CENTRAL MESSAGE that you want your media
event to communicate—consistent with your broader strategic
communications strategy. (See Chapter 3, "Strategic Media
Plans.")

Your message should be contained in one phrase; following
are some examples of simple messages:

- The incinerator will cause cancer.
- Don't tear down the old Sand Inn.
- Gov. Idlebrain does not support education.
- Put 100 more police officers on the streets.
- Stop hunting whales.
- Use cloth grocery sacks.
- Don't drink and drive.
- Vote yes on Amendment 1.
- It's the economy, Stupid.

Once you've clarified your message, you should create
a couple of sound bites to communicate it to journalists. A sound
bite is a quotable statement supporting your message. And depending on the length of interviews you expect to have, you
should develop up to a half-dozen simple points to support your
message—each with one or more sound bites. (See Chapter 16, "Interviews.")

As Thoreau wrote, simplify, simplify, simplify. Journalists—television journalists, in particular—rarely confuse their audience with complex information, which might prompt some lazy people to change the channel. For this reason, the script of a newscast is generally written with the assumption that viewers comprehend at the sixth-grade level. To fit into this format, your message needs to be simple, clear, and easily understood.

As you develop your simple message for an event, be clear about what you want to accomplish. Maybe you want to awaken the public by sending frightening news. Maybe you want your community to know that the mayor is ignoring crimes in your neighborhood. Or maybe you want to draw attention to a piece of legislation addressing the problem.

Don't combine two events in one. For example, there's no reason to release a report about the benefits of recycling cans and announce the kickoff of a ballot initiative mandating recycling of cans at the same press conference. It's better to plan a press strategy involving the release of the report later in order to draw further attention to the ballot initiative.

After you have developed your message, build your media event around it. Everything about your event should help communicate this message—the site, the speakers, the sound bites, the signs, the images associated with the event itself—every possible detail.

9

Brainstorm
Stunt Ideas

With television more and more dominant in our society, words—especially written words—are weak and getting weaker as a tool for communicating. To reach most people, you have to package your message in an image or symbol and stage an event.

To create an event, consider assembling a group (of about a dozen people) for a brainstorming session. I'm not a big fan of doing tasks in groups, but this really works.

Turn to Chapter 1, which describes categories of media stunts that have generated news coverage and lists examples of how citizens have tailored each category of stunt to fit their issue. Each category has been used by activists representing completely different causes.

In some cases, you'll be able to take an idea directly from Chapter 1 and use it for your cause. In other cases, the ideas and examples will serve as models for you to adapt and to stimulate your own creativity.

Read each generic stunt category (for example, costumes) aloud. If appropriate, read specific examples of how this category of stunt was used. Then write down everyone's ideas for adapting it to your cause. Write down every idea conceived during the brainstorm without criticizing it, without getting more details, and without exploring the pros and cons. As you think of ideas, do not get bogged down in logistics such as where the event would be held and who would bring props.

You can find at least one goof in your group to execute a media stunt, like this police officer doing the "twist" to encourage kids to wear seatbelts. You could bet that none of his colleagues in the background would ever hula hoop for the media. Photo: Dave Buresh, Denver Post.

Say, for example, you want to come up with an event to convey your message that people should contribute food for a canned food drive. You would open this book to Chapter 1 and start reading through the categories of media events, looking for ones that fit your needs. The first category is "Cameras Love Costumes."

How could you use a costume? Perhaps you could create a can costume and visit a school. The next category is "Dramatize a Popular Expression." How about making a giant toilet for people to drop off their canned food items (Go to the "can.")? Then you go on to the next category. . . . After all the ideas are in, go back and decide what's doable and what will be most newsworthy.

People frequently tell me that they'd like to stop staging boring press events, but their organization is not composed of juveniles willing to dress in costumes, confront officials, take off some of their clothes, and so on. I do not accept this as an excuse for not staging creative media events. In most cases, all you need is one or two people who are willing to look stupid. All the rest can stand on the sidelines and smirk, or help in some other way. It's your job to find the person in your group who is willing to do what needs to be done. There's a clown or two in every group. They may be shy, or they may think that being a media prop takes more talent than it really does. You just have to coax this person out of the closet. There's plenty of undiscovered goofiness out there. And it pays off. It gets attention and, as Saul Alinsky wrote, it's almost impossible to counterattack ridicule.

10

The Best Times
to Get Coverage

You can't stop the gas line under Sweetkids Elementary from exploding—setting fire to hundreds of Halloween lunch boxes and eclipsing the press conference you are holding at the same time. But staging your event on certain days at certain times will increase your chances of being covered.

For Best Coverage, Monday Through Thursday

Thanks to the Internet, and all-news networks like CNN, MSNBC, and Fox, important news is distributed as quickly as reporters can do their job—day or night. However, for most news—particularly news from local activists and nonprofit groups—this "24-hour news cycle" does *not* apply. So you need to be savvy about when to release your news or stage your photo opportunity (photo op).

Reporters generally work long but regular hours. Media outlets pare down their staffs substantially on weekends and after deadlines on weekdays, leaving only a couple of reporters (usually young ones) in the newsroom, instead of dozens. Barring exceptions (read on), it's best to stage your event Monday through Thursday between 10 A.M. and 2 P.M.

Because of traffic and deadlines, an event after 3 P.M. is a headache for most reporters. Only the most newsworthy events will be covered in the late afternoon or evening. "Timing is everything," says Tom Donahue, Miami bureau chief for CBS News. "They might have something real interesting to say, but if they have a press conference at 6 P.M., we can't do much with it."

If your event is powerful and relevant enough, it will be covered no matter when you hold it and regardless of routine deadlines. But only rarely, if ever, will your event fall into the must-be-covered-no-matter-what category.

If you're tailoring your event for local TV news and it's got excellent visual components, stage it when the news airs on TV (usually noon, 5 P.M., or 10 P.M.), allowing local TV news to broadcast live at the scene. You should also consider aiming for live local coverage between 6 A.M. and 8 A.M. If you are targeting local news, you should know that an increasingly large number of the news stories are live, and you should try to accommodate this format in your event.

If you hold a weekend event, Saturday afternoon is a terrible time for print media because the first editions of Sunday's paper are out Saturday morning. If you want to hold an event on the weekend, stage it on Sunday for coverage on TV Sunday night and in Monday's newspaper. Sunday can be a slow news day, increasing your odds of being covered.

Staging an event on Friday is not a good idea because Saturday's paper usually has fewer pages, so there is less space for news; and many reporters are busy on Friday writing for Sunday's paper. Also, fewer people read Saturday's paper or watch the evening news on Friday night.

However, you should consider Friday for a news event if you want to *avoid* coverage. Notice how big newsmakers, like the government or corporations, use Friday afternoon to release damaging information that they *don't* want covered.

Remember, it's often best to hook your event to issues that journalists are already covering. (See Chapter 21, "Hook Your Story to Breaking News.")

Hook Your Event to Stories in the News

By hooking your event to news that's already being covered, you do not have to convince reporters that it's a good time to cover your issue—because it's already on their agendas. You simply have to persuade them to cover your perspective. A stunt or media event offers them the opportunity to do this—and a way to *illustrate* their stories.

For example, opponents of the death penalty have a tough time attracting media attention. Their numbers are small and their cause unpopular. But a simple rally on the day that convicted Oklahoma City bomber Timothy McVeigh was sentenced to die attracted dozens of reporters around a small band of sign-carrying activists. One man, carrying a sign that read "WHAT WOULD JESUS DO?" was mobbed by reporters.

Try to determine if your media event is strong enough to stand on its own or if it needs to ride the coattails of issues. If you've got Dustin Hoffman leading a caravan of 20,000 farmers in tractors to the state capitol, you can pick your time and date. If all you've got is three activists in penguin suits and you're trying to draw attention to the slaughter of penguins, you'd better wait until something related to penguin killing is already in the news.

Many activists and organizations try to connect their issue to giant news hooks, like the arrival of the president to their town. A circus of stunters creates such intense competition that many are shut out of the news. Consider elevating your prop above the crowd to make it stand out, or—better—pick another date.

For Photographs, Try Monday, Tuesday, or Sunday Morning

Newspaper photographers are least busy Monday and Tuesday after 10 A.M. Wednesday and Thursday are busier because photographers are shooting for Sunday's paper. Friday is a bad day because Saturday's paper contains fewer photos. Weekdays before a holiday can also be hectic for photographers and writers alike.

Sunday morning, before the afternoon sports trauma, can be an excellent time because photographers are looking for shots for Monday's paper and there's generally not a lot happening. Notice how many shots of running races appear in Monday's paper. (See Chapter 26, "Influence Newspaper Photographers.")

Dodge Busy News Days and the "Sweeps"

The slower the news day, the better your chances of being covered. Logically, then, you want to avoid days when you know a major media event is scheduled (such as Super Bowls, court trials, elections).

Nielsen periodically rates television programs based on how many viewers they attract. (Arbitron rates radio programs.) The stakes are enormous: Programs with higher ratings charge higher advertising rates. Networks respond to the "sweeps," as the ratings are called, by running extra promotions.

For television news, the sweeps month translates into maximum blood, supreme pathos, and consummate sentimentality. You'll hear the stations promoting—with live gusto—upcoming television news segments. Some of these segments have been weeks or months in the making. It can be hard for cause-related events to compete. Don't be "swept" under the rug. Find out when the sweeps happen and avoid them.

Be Flexible

Alter your plans if developments in the news dictate that you do so. For example, when I was working for Greenpeace, I planned for months to release a report in Ft. Lauderdale, Florida, exposing that Florida would be among the top pollution-generating states in the United States by 2012. The report described how Florida's pollution from coal-fired power plants could be contributing to global warming, which could cause catastrophic climatic changes worldwide. The report outlined anecdotal evidence that impacts of global warming—including droughts, floods, hurricanes, and temperature increases—were already detectable worldwide.

We planned to deliver our report in a coffin to a major power company near Miami. I flew to Florida on Monday, and just hours after the plane landed, an unseasonal tropical storm named Gordon hit. Our plan to release our report Thursday no longer seemed viable because all the major news media were fixated on the storm, which was causing serious damage. The news media were particularly obsessed with the saga of a giant barge that had become stranded right off the beach.

We changed our plans, deciding that raising a possible link between the storm and global warming was not only legitimate but consistent with our point. Instead of delivering the report in a coffin to the power company, which was a fairly dubious event in the first place, we placed a banner over the coffin—"Gordon Early Warning of Global Warming?"—and dragged it to the beach where the barge was stuck. This worked. Our coffin was greeted by local TV news cameras and print and radio reporters.

The storm was our hook, and suddenly global warming, a complex problem that's difficult for the mainstream media to cover, was news. If we had waited for the storm to pass and proceeded with our original plans to deliver the report to the power company, we'd have been lucky to have attracted any media attention at all, especially on Miami local TV news, which is known for its thirst for mayhem.

Sample Timetable for Organizing a Media Event

Here's a five-month timetable for media work leading up to an event. *You don't need five months.* In fact, with one day's notice, I've organized stunts related to political issues that have received national press coverage. Other types of events—theater productions, art shows, and the like—require many months of planning. In any case, the earlier you get started with publicity, the better your chances of letting the world know about your event. (Details about how to execute the following activities are all described in the following Part Three chapters.)

Five Months in Advance. Clarify your goals, target audience, and message. If you're organizing an event, settle on an appropriate visual image. Select a location. Obtain a permit, if necessary. Compile a media list, which you should augment as your media outreach proceeds.

Four Months in Advance. Write and distribute a "calendar item" for monthly magazines and other outlets that need to be notified long in advance. Send a press kit, including feature ideas, and follow up with a phone call. Begin your outreach to media sponsors if appropriate.

Two Months in Advance. If you're planning a cultural or art event, arrange for the artists to perform somewhere for free—at a school or senior center—during the week prior to the show's opening. This offers the media another way to cover an art show as news.

Six Weeks in Advance. Distribute a "guest availability" to talk radio and television talk shows, including morning local TV shows. Follow up with phone calls. Make sure all spokespeople are prepared for interviews. They should practice delivering sound bites and answering questions.

One Month in Advance. Distribute your "calendar listing" to daily and weekly news outlets and newsletters. Make sure you've got the calendar editor's name right and make follow-up calls to make sure your item is received. Include photos or art for publication in calendars. Call feature writers at daily newspapers with story ideas.

Two Weeks in Advance. If your artists are performing at a pro bono event, distribute a press release about the performance to daily news outlets two days before the pro bono event occurs. Highlight anything unique or highly visual in your press release. Make follow-up calls two days before the performance.

One Week in Advance. Write your news release for daily newspapers, television news shows, and other daily outlets.

Three Days in Advance. Distribute your release and follow up with phone calls. Assemble a press kit for the event.

One Day in Advance. Call all daily news outlets and critics.

Day of the Event. Place a reminder call to TV stations and journalists who told you they plan to attend. At the event, distribute media kits and assign one or two people to sign in journalists and help them obtain any information they need.

11

Where to Stage a Media Event

THE LOCATION OF YOUR MEDIA event should provide an image that helps communicate the message you are sending. For example, if you are denouncing a local developer, you should probably stage your event in front of the developer's offices (or the site of a particular development) with the company's sign and logo and *yours* as a backdrop. (For extra conflict, tape a sign with your message over your opponent's sign.)

An on-location event conference makes much better sense than holing up in a nondescript room somewhere. It adds a sense of action—even if you are simply holding an otherwise boring news conference. Other factors, however, may weigh against your staging an event at the developer's office. Ask yourself these questions:

Is the Location Convenient? Most news organizations are understaffed, and reporters are extremely busy. On top of that, many are lazy. Select a location that is close to the downtown area. An artist I know once spent months creating a replica of the deadly plutonium contained in U.S. nuclear bombs. It was an extraordinary visual. But she displayed it in an obscure plaza about an hour away from the nearest news outlet. Since the "exhibit" was definitely not on any reporter's "must-cover" list and the location was inconvenient, she received little media coverage. The news media will come to you wherever you are if you've got a story they want badly enough. The problem is, you'll seldom have such a story. So you should pick a location that's easy for journalists to access.

Is Your Site Commonly Used for Media Events? Most cities have a spot that's well-known to journalists as the Place of the Protesters. Usually it's the state capitol steps. Avoid this location if possible.

If Your Event Is Outdoors, Do You Have a Backup Location? It's always better to hold a news conference outside, and more often than not a little rain or bad weather won't hurt your chances of being covered. But you should have backup plans in case severe weather strikes. It could be best to reschedule your event, as stories about severe weather may cut deeply into TV news.

Do You Need a Permit? For most events on private property, permits are not required. For public property, permit requirements vary substantially from municipality to municipality. Generally, sidewalks are less regulated than parks and city squares. If you do not obstruct the sidewalk (that is, if people can walk around you and your props on the sidewalk), a permit is not usually needed, although some cities demand a permit if you are going to place anything on the sidewalk. For larger public spaces (parks, the capitol steps, and so on), a permit is usually required for any demonstration.

Often you will be asked to provide proof of insurance or, if you have none, to buy insurance for your event. You should be able to persuade permit offices to waive this requirement if your event is related to politics and therefore protected by the First Amendment. It helps if you are not selling anything, including food, at your event.

What About Staging an Event Without a Permit? If you stage an event on public property without a permit, you won't be breaking the law until the police ask you to leave. Thus it's possible to complete your event before you're told to move. If asked, you can leave and not be arrested. Also, with the media present, the police may choose not to bother you.

If you set up on private property without permission, you can be charged with trespassing. But again, usually you will first be asked to leave voluntarily.

Sample Permit Application

File with: Capitol Complex
                                        Attn. Permit Manager

Date of Application _____
Date of Event Scheduled _____   Time _____

Name of Organization Holding Event _____
Contact Person _____ Phone_____
Address _____
E-mail _____

Please provide a detailed description of the event, including sales, use of tables, structures, tents, and so on. Attach additional pages as necessary.

Attach proof of insurance in the amount of $500,000 showing that your organization is insured against personal injury or property damage. (Requests are considered for waiver of this provision.)

I have read all attached rules and regulations on the reverse side of this application and agree to comply with all requirements. I further agree to hold the government harmless for any injury resulting from the use of the property.

Waiver of insurance requested_____

Waiver of $100 damage deposit requested _____

Signature   Date

Where Do You Obtain Permits? For sidewalks, the local police department is usually the place to go. Or start your run through the bureaucracy by calling the county clerk. For parks and city squares, call the city parks department, the maintenance office for the capitol, or possibly the city manager's office. If you request permits repeatedly, make friends with the workers in the permit office. Sending them a thank-you letter is helpful, as is making sure you clean the site carefully before you leave.

Tips for Creating a
Great Photo

As you select a location for your media event, think about how photographers will view it.

- Note the background. Make sure that it's not distracting or noisy, and select a background that's relevant to your event and message.
- Outside is better than inside. The light is usually better, and outdoor photos suggest more action and spontaneity.
- Try to have the sun shining on the objects you want photographed.
- Sidelighting is the biggest headache for photographers; backlighting is second best lighting.
- Make sure signs or banners are readable from a distance.
- Don't leave items lying around that you don't want photographed. "On my hunger strike, I told reporters I was drinking juice, so it wasn't a secret," says Tim Ream, an environmental activist from Portland, Oregon. "But the natural inclination for photographers was to shoot the juice bottles I had. So I put them aside."
- Consider putting your banner message on your clothes in case your signs and banners are removed or cropped from the photo.
- Handmade signs are better than mass-produced ones. They add a human and artistic touch.
- Remember, photographers like action shots—not set-up arrangements. But if you see photographers, turn your signs in their direction.
- Create your event so a photographer has few (or no!) options to take photographs that you would rather *not* see in the news.

12

Media Sponsors

IF YOU HAVE THE RIGHT event, try to persuade a media organization to "sponsor" it. A media sponsor can be a tremendous help: advertising your event, covering it live, selling tickets, printing programs, and more. Entertainment-oriented and noncontroversial events—a run for hunger, senior appreciation day at the zoo, an arts festival, a concert—are most likely to attract sponsors. In exchange, you need to offer your media sponsor something: space for your sponsor's banner at your event (and on your Website), free passes to your event, its name and logo printed in your event's program or on tickets, time for a spokesperson representing your sponsor to say a few words at your event, and more.

Sponsorship agreements can vary tremendously, from simple to complicated. "I may just send my van out with hula hoops," says Michelle Dirks, director of marketing and promotions for WJMK-FM, a radio station in Chicago.

Most news organizations shy away from sponsoring political events because they don't want to offend any of their viewers, listeners, or readers. Some radio stations, however, may sponsor an event with a political message if their audience (or "market share") is likely to support it. Because there are dozens of radio stations in most media markets (versus only a handful of TV stations), their audiences are highly specific; thus they don't have to try to appeal to everyone. For example, one local radio station whose listeners are mostly college students and yuppies sent its van to a Planned Parenthood Valentine's Day event involving the free distribution of condoms to passersby.

The key to landing a media sponsor is offering an event its audience will appreciate. "Do I want to be involved with an all-night bike-a-thon?" asks Michelle Dirks at WJMK-FM. "My listeners have kids. They have to be up at six in the morning. I know that my listeners aren't going to be passionate about certain things."

Keep in mind that most media organizations sponsor events for business reasons—not out of the goodness of their hearts. Think about how your event might boost their marketing strategy.

"We compare information from organizations with our current marketing strategy," says Angie Clark, newspaper in education manager for the *St. Louis Post-Dispatch.* "Based on our strategy at the time, we evaluate the event."

Tips for Signing Up a Media Sponsor

- Try to make your event known around town before you seek media sponsors. An event that's already generating attention will be more attractive to sponsors.
- Zero in on who will attend your event. Then approach media outlets that serve this group of people. For example, if your event will be attended by teenagers, approach teen radio stations for sponsorships.
- Prepare a short proposal (one or two pages) for potential sponsors, describing your event, its history, and who will attend it.
- In your written proposal, be clear on what the media outlet will get from you and what you want in return. Request meeting to talk about it.
- To gauge interest, send simultaneous sponsorship proposals to different media outlets, outlining both what you can offer and what you hope to receive in return. Then you can decide which offer is best for you. However, it's *not* a good idea to pit one media outlet against another in a bidding war.
- You may want to offer a sponsor the "first opportunity" to accept your proposal before you shop around.
- If possible, send sponsorship proposals to outlets at least two months in advance. Address them *by name* to the promotions director or other appropriate person. You'll find

that potential sponsors put different staff with different titles in charge of promotions. Find out the correct name and
title at the media organization that you are targeting. "If it's
a contest that might help build circulation, it would fall under consumer communications," says Angie Clark at the *St.
Louis Post-Dispatch*. "If it's cause-related or good will, it
would fall under community relations."

- You may be able to ask an outlet to provide refreshments,
  which it might be able to obtain from an advertiser.
- Consider offering the potential sponsor the right to sell banner space, which it can connect to advertising sales.
- If it's OK with your sponsors, sign up multiple sponsors for
  one event. A sponsor may request that no competitive media (for example, another TV station) be allowed to sponsor
  the event.
- If you plan to sell tickets to your event in advance, you can
  offer your media sponsor the right to sell them. Your sponsor, in turn, can sell a retail store the rights to sell the advance
  tickets. (This is what's happening when you hear on the radio that tickets to an event are on sale at, say, a record store.)
- Make the event fun for journalists who come. Invite their
  kids and have food.
- Most community groups have the best luck with radio stations. For smaller events, it's best to determine who will attend and which news media they consume. Television stations generally sponsor only major events.

Cause-Related Marketing

A media sponsorship is actually a type of cause-related marketing
(CRM), which is a marketing partnership between a for-profit corporation and a nonprofit organization. Examples include:

- Levi Strauss & Company partnered with the Health Education Board of Scotland and sponsored TV commercials with
  the line: "Condoms . . . what to wear when you're not
  wearing jeans."
- For its part, the Lee jeans company sponsors an annual
  "Lee National Denim Day." For $5, you sign up for the

"freedom" to wear jeans to work. Funds go to the Susan G. Komen Breast Cancer Foundation.

- Cadbury, the British chocolate maker, placed the World Wildlife Fund's logo on one of its chocolate bars and donated cash to WWF for each bar sold.

Cause-related marketing is as varied as your imagination, but it's based on the idea that a for-profit business will benefit (make more money, attract more customers, and so on) by associating itself with the good work of a nonprofit. In return, nonprofit groups get advertising help, more donations, volunteers, or other benefits. In theory, it's a win/win arrangement.

Even if you don't engage in cause-related marketing yourself, you should beware of it: Some businesses try to polish their corporate images by associating with a "good cause," when in reality their business practices are harming the community (for example, a company that pollutes "partners" with an environmental group to make the company look environmentally friendly).

13

Media Lists

You NEED TO ASSEMBLE A list of journalists who might be interested in covering your media event and your cause. Once your list is in place, you can access it when you want to distribute a news release or call a reporter to suggest a news story. With all your media contacts listed in one location, contacting journalists can be done efficiently and quickly.

There's no single correct way to organize a media list. In fact, what I present in this chapter is probably more elaborate than most community groups need. But I hope to inspire you to gather as much information as possible about news outlets and journalists. This will pay off for you and your organization in the long run.

The media list of many nonprofits consists of a dozen or so major media in their area, including three or four TV stations, one or two daily newspapers, one alternative weekly newspaper, a news service like the Associated Press, two to four radio news programs, and a handful of talk-radio shows.

Each news outlet usually has one contact name, fax number, phone number, and an e-mail address. The contacts for TV stations are usually assignment editors. For newspapers and news radio, they're reporters. For talk radio, they're producers.

The following is a sample skeletal media list entry:

Name of News Outlet   Orlando Sentinel
First Name of Journalist   Katey
Last Name of Journalist   Forell

Title of Journalist	Business Reporter
Phone Number	xxx-222-3434
Fax Number	xxx-222-3535
E-mail Address	kforell@cnn.com

A media list with this basic information will work for many community organizations, particularly if they've made a strategic decision *not* to make media outreach much of a priority. Such a list with a dozen or so entries will allow an organization to do a respectable job of reaching out to the local news media, especially if other tips in this book (for example, respect deadlines, follow up a news release with a phone call) are mastered.

But a skeletal media list will not allow nonprofits to excel at media outreach and *long-term communications*—reaching the maximum number of people with your message and affecting how they perceive your organization and issues.

A bare-bones list can be disastrous for an organization when staff depart, taking along all the undocumented information in their heads. Make a serious, long-term commitment to getting the word out. Take extra time to create a stellar media list with detailed information.

How to Get a Media List

The best way to begin is to call citizen groups that work on a cause similar to yours and ask for their media list. You can take what they've done and build on it.

If you can't get help from another organization or perhaps a friend who does public relations, turn to old-fashioned reference books, like the *Bacon's* directories. These are costly, but you can use the dead-tree versions at the library. These sources are better than free, online media lists (like www.congress.org) because they have more detailed information about staff journalists, including their titles, direct phone numbers, and often e-mail addresses. If you use a free online media list, you will most likely have to call the main number of each news outlet and ask for the names of the types of reporters you want to reach (for local TV news, for example, ask who's the assignment editor?). Finally, if you can't find online sources for your area, look in your phone book's yellow pages under "news." (See Resources, "Lists of News Outlets and Journalists.")

Over time, you'll develop relationships with journalists. These contacts will be of the most value in the long run. However, you don't need personal contacts in the media to be an effective publicist. Just act professionally, learn the simple tips in this book, and you will do well.

Keep your media list current. You should update it thoroughly every six months by calling each news outlet to make sure personnel have not changed. Then if you have to act quickly, you needn't scramble to make sure your information is accurate.

Maintain a list that matches your needs and your computer power. It's best to have a software program that can retrieve your media data sorted according to any of the categories you set up, as described next. Those lagging behind in the technology race can use a binder with pages that can be changed easily.

How to Organize a Media List

I've purchased a CD-ROM that allows me to access reporters by city, name, beat, title, whatever. It's great but expensive and unnecessary for most community organizers who work in one city or a few states.

Most activists need to divide their media lists first by *media market* and second by *categories of news outlets* in each market. This way, you can target major metropolitan areas (such as the San Francisco market) across the country and have detailed information on the area's news outlets, including the bureaus of national news outlets. (For example, your Chicago list should include the Chicago bureaus of National Public Radio, CNN, FOX Network News, and so on.)

A media market can be defined as a geographic area with its own television stations and is named after the largest city or cities in it. The broadcasting area of a TV station may extend to a few cities. For example, Minneapolis and St. Paul are in a single media market. So are Seattle and Tacoma and Tampa, St. Petersburg, and Sarasota. One media market may have numerous radio stations, daily newspapers, and other media. In addition, some newspapers or radio stations reach more than one media market. For example, a newspaper may be distributed to an entire state, and there may be multiple television markets within one state. National news outlets, including industry newsletters, should be grouped into a "national market."

Usually, however, a media market has at least one news outlet from each of these major categories: (1) daily newspapers, (2) weekly newspapers or magazines, (3) quarterly, monthly, or fortnightly newspapers or magazines, (4) daily television news, (5) television public affairs programs, including national TV talk shows and television "news magazines," (6) news radio, (7) talk radio, (8) pop radio, (9) news services and bureaus of national news outlets, (10) Web-based news outlets ("e-zines"), and (11) freelance journalists.

Keep your entries standardized so that groups of news outlets can be retrieved from your list. If you're promoting your event or cause in more than one media market, develop separate lists of outlets for each. If you are a local community organizer in, say, Portland, the bulk of the news outlets on your list will be located in one media market (that is, the Portland TV-viewing environs). Following are two sample list entries:

Sample Television News Media List Entry

Market:	New York City
Type of News Outlet:	local television news
Name or Call Letters of News Outlet:	WNYW TV FOX
Channel:	5
First Name of Journalist:	Jane
Last Name of Journalist:	Reporter
Title:	Assignment Editor
Street Address:	1234 Broadway
City:	New York
State:	NY
Zip:	10012
Phone:	212–xxx–2222
FAX:	212–xxx–3333
E-Mail:	Jay@wnyw.com
Deadline:	3:30 P.M.
Format:	Live anchors, live and taped stories

Comments: Typical local news show
History: 2/97 Called expressing
                                       interest in any rallies
                                       against media
                                       sensationalism.
                                   7/97 Receptive to our
                                       throw-the-TV-in-the-
                                       Dumpster event, but
                                       did not send crew.

Sample Print Media List Entry

Market: Los Angeles and National
Type of News Outlet: daily newspaper
Name or Call Letters of News Outlet: *Los Angeles Times*
Channel:
First Name of Journalist: Jay
Last Name of Journalist Reporter:
Title: Media Critic
Street Address: Times Mirror Square
City: Los Angeles
State: CA
Zip: 90053
Phone: 213–xxx–7000
FAX: 213–xxx–7968
E-mail: Jay@latimes.com
Deadline: 3:30 P.M.
Format: Major metropolitan daily,
                                               plus national coverage
Comments: Very unreceptive to
                                               media literacy report
                                               4/97.
History: Called for a comment
                                               on citizen access to
                                               editorial pages 8/97.
                                               Wrote an excellent
                                               piece on 2/1/98.

After the name or call letters of a news outlet, make sure you specify AM or FM for radio. Also, note the power of the signal. Fifty-thousand-watt stations and above can cover a whole state, whereas 2,000-watt stations have weak signals that carry only a few miles.

Keep journalist titles standardized so you can retrieve them together if need be. Be as specific as possible. For example, don't just use the title "reporter." Specify what kind, such as "business reporter." Here are some common titles appearing in my media list: assignment editor, anchor, general reporter, environment reporter, editorial page editor, cartoonist, columnist, photo editor, news director, community calendar editor, talk-show host, and producer.

In the format section for radio and TV, describe the number of guests, whether the show is live or taped, whether calls are accepted, and so on.

The comments section is useful for recording anything unusual about the outlet. Is this a specialty, alternative, or industry outlet? For broadcast outlets, describe the slant of the show, including the personality of the host, if applicable, and the typical topics.

To provide your group with "media memory," record in the history section all coverage your organization receives from each outlet, including instances when a reporter calls you and how you were treated. This may be too much to do thoroughly in the heat of day-to-day work, but it's worth a try, particularly if a noteworthy media interaction takes place.

In Chapter 15, "Distributing News Release," read the section called "Whom to Contact at News Outlets" for a description of the types of reporters that you should include in your media list.

14

News Releases

A NEWS RELEASE IS THE vehicle for alerting the media to your event. It's a brief written explanation of your plans.

"I might have thirty seconds to spend on a news release," says Paul Day, a reporter for KCNC-TV, the CBS affiliate in Denver, adding that he has to be "hit over the head with ideas" and that the important information should "leap off the page."

"When I get to the office in the morning, I already have 20 or so news releases waiting, most of them dull," says Claus Kleber, chief U.S. correspondent for KRD, German public television.

"I get a hundred or more news releases a day just myself, and not all of them are in English," says Dee Lane, Portland editor of *The Oregonian.*

"What it all comes down to is the headline," says Steve Chavis, former news director at KBCO-FM, a Boulder radio station.

With some creativity and basic pointers, your release can stand out from the pile.

The best way to learn to write a news release is to look at examples. I've got four below, following this list of tips.

Tips for Writing a News Release

- A news release should usually not be longer than one page, especially if you are distributing it by fax. If reporters want more information than you can fit on one page, they will ask you for it, and you should have it ready. If you e-mail your release, you need not be bound by the one-page rule, but you should still keep it short. E-mailed releases should link to your Website. And you should have other information (photos, reports, bios, and so on) available in both electronic and dead-tree form.

- In the top left corner, type "For Immediate Release."
- In the top right corner, type the date.
- Below "For Immediate Release," type names and phone numbers of two contacts. Make sure these contacts can be easily reached by phone.
- For an e-mailed release, you should consider putting the contact information and date at the bottom of the release. This way, the reporter will see the headline in the preview screen on the computer, rather than contact information and date.
- Use a larger font for your headline than for the text of the release.
- Type a headline on the release. I usually write two separate headlines on a total of up to six lines.
- Try one sentence per paragraph; at most, use three.
- Write the release like a news story with the information in descending order of importance. Use short sentences and no jargon.
- Spend 75 percent of your time writing the headline and first paragraph.
- Your release should answer who, what, where, when, why, and how. If you prefer, you can write these words on the left side of the page and answer them on the right side.
- Emphasize what's unique: the first, the biggest, and so on.
- If your event will have good visuals, describe them prominently!
- Type "—30—" or "###" at the end of your release. This is how journalists mark the end of news copy.
- Type "MORE" at the end of page 1 if your release is two pages.
- Distribute your release on the letterhead of an organization even if a coalition of groups is writing it.
- Briefly describe your organization in the last paragraph of your news release—with a link to your Website.
- The two key points are to keep it short and write a good headline.

Some public relations experts use numerous styles of re-leases—for events, background information, a calendar listing. One basic release, however, will work fine. What's important is what's written on the release and who receives it at a news organization.

You may, however, wish to modify your news release slightly for a news advisory (see below) or a calendar listing. (See Chapter 30, "Use Community Calendars and Public Service Announcements.")

Five sample news releases follow on the next five pages.

Five Sample News Releases

Contact: Jason Salzman (303) 292-1524   September 26, 2002
Jeff Galusha   (802) 598-6426

Armed with a Pig Nose and a Giant "Pentagon Pig," Ben of Ben and Jerry's to lead "Snort-In" Against Iraq War

Massive Pig Vehicle Rolls into Chicago for Anti-War Protest

In the 1960s, political activists held sit-ins and teach-ins against the Vietnam War. Now, they're holding a "snort-in" against the Iraq War.

Donning pig noses and led by Ben Cohen, co-founder of Ben and Jerry's, activists will gather in Chicago to "snort" at the prospect of invading Iraq.

The snort-in will take place Thursday, September 26, at 1:30 p.m. in Lincoln Park, 2021 North Stockton Drive (in the picnic area just north of Café Brauer, just north of the zoo and the farm).

Joining the snorting protestors will be a 12-foot Pentagon "Pig," representing the defense budget. This strange vehicle pulls two small pigs—proportionately representing America's small budgets for "Education" and "World Hunger."

"We plan to snort at the Administration's intention to invade Iraq," said Ben Cohen, President of the TrueMajority. "This is not the time for the American people to wallow. All of us should speak out against the war."
The snort-in is sponsored by the TrueMajority, a nonprofit organization founded by Ben Cohen. Twice a month, at critical moments, TrueMajority members receive a short e-mail alert about an important issue pending in Washington. With the click of a mouse, members can send a fax to their Congressperson. The TrueMajority is currently empowering citizens to speak out against the Iraq war.

For more information, see www.truemajority.com.

--30--

Especially when promoting a stunt or photo op, emphasize the visual elements of your event and any involvement by celebrities in the headline. And highlight the time and location. CREDIT: TRUEMAJORITY.ORG

ENVIRONMENTAL WORKING GROUP

FOR IMMEDIATE RELEASE: May 15, 2002

CONTACT: Bill Walker, EWG, (510) 444-0973
Liza Pike, EMS West, (415) 561-2325

DIRTY AIR A CAUSE OF DEATH FOR 9,300 CALIFORNIANS EACH YEAR
Report Details Deaths, Illnesses, Other Costs of Pollution in Each County

OAKLAND, May 15 – Airborne soot and dust causes or contributes to the deaths of more Californians than traffic accidents, homicide and AIDS combined, according to a new report released today by Environmental Working Group (EWG).

EWG's analysis of state data found that respiratory illnesses caused or made worse by microscopic particles of soot and dust – technically, particulate matter or PM – are responsible for more than 9,300 deaths, thousands of hospital visits, hundreds of thousands of asthma attacks and millions of missed work days each year. "Particle Civics: How Cleaner Air in California Will Save Lives and Save Money," available at www.ewg.org, not only details the public health impacts in each county in the state, but for the first time puts a price tag on the annual cost of particulate pollution.

"There's an overwhelming scientific consensus that particulate pollution kills people," said Renee Sharp, EWG analyst and principal author of the report. "Cleaning up the air is as important to public health and safety as wearing seatbelts."

State scientists have proposed tougher new air pollution standards that would save about 6,500 lives and half a billion dollars a year, but they face strong opposition from a coalition of oil companies and automakers who have contributed more than $175,000 to Gov. Gray Davis's re-election campaign. The Davis-appointed Air Resources Board will vote on the proposed standards next month, and the decision will be closely watched as the U.S. EPA prepares to set new federal particulate standards.

Particulate air pollution is most severe in the greater Los Angeles metropolitan area and the San Joaquin Valley. But statewide, 55 of 58 counties have average annual particulate levels that exceed the proposed state standards. EWG also found:

• Each year, particulate air pollution is responsible for more than 16,000 hospital or emergency room admissions, at an estimated health care cost of $132 million.

• PM-related illnesses cause Californians to miss almost 5 million work days a year, a loss to the state's economy of more than $880 million.

• Cutting particulate pollution to levels recommended by state scientists will reduce PM-triggered deaths by at least 69 percent, asthma attacks by 57 percent, hospital visits by 56 percent and cases of chronic bronchitis by 58 percent.

EWG California • 1904 Franklin St., Ste. 515 • Oakland, CA 94612 • Tel. (510) 444-0973 • Fax (510) 444-0982
california@ewg.org • www.ewg.org/california

A complex report on air pollution is brilliantly summed up in one simple sentence, which is the lead paragraph of this news release. Note that the full report is available on the Internet.
CREDIT: ENVIRONMENTAL WORKING GROUP

Press Release
For Immediate Release – February 14, 2001
Contact: Betsy Leondar-Wright
(617) 423-2148 x13

Bill Gates, Sr., George Soros, Steven Rockefeller, 100 Others Oppose Estate Tax Repeal

Repealing the estate tax "would be a terrible mistake," equivalent to "choosing the 2020 Olympic team by picking the eldest sons of the gold-medal winners in the 2000 Olympics."-- Warren Buffett in this morning's New York Times

Over 100 prominent business and philanthropic leaders today issued a joint statement, covered on the front page of today's *New York Times*, opposing President Bush's proposed repeal of the estate tax. Signers include **William H. Gates, Sr.; George Soros**; Steven C. Rockefeller and other members of the **Rockefeller family; Ben Cohen; Paul Newman**; other philanthropists; and members of **Responsible Wealth** with both new entrepreneurial wealth and old inherited wealth. (See attached statement and partial signer list.)

> **Conference call:** Responsible Wealth will host an opportunity for journalists to interview **Bill Gates, Sr.,** Chuck Collins of United for a Fair Economy, and other critics of estate tax repeal on **Tuesday, February 20 at 1 p.m. EST**. Some signers of the statement are also available for one-on-one interviews.

"Repealing the estate tax would leave an unfortunate legacy for America's future generations," the signers warn. Repeal would undermine philanthropy and "would enrich the heirs of America's millionaires and billionaires while hurting families who struggle to make ends meet." The signers say, "Let's fix the estate tax, not repeal it." For more information, visit www.responsiblewealth.org.

Responsible Wealth is a national network of businesspeople, investors and affluent Americans concerned about deepening economic inequality and advocating widespread prosperity.

###

To register for Tuesday's conference call, please call (617) 423-2148 x13 or return this form by e-mail (bleondar-wright@ufenet.org) or by fax, (617) 423-0196. Registration deadline Friday 2/16. We will send you instructions for joining the call.

NAME: _____

AFFILIATION: _____ PHONE: (____) ____ - _____

E-MAIL _____ FAX: (____) ____ - _____

You don't need to write a long news release to make your point. This release offers reporters the opportunity to interview spokespeople during a conference call. CREDIT: RESPONSIBLE WEALTH COALITION

Citizens Against Pepsi

Contact: Aaron Toso   (303) 292-1524   February 4, 2003
(303) 359-xxxx cell

Citizens Call on Denver School Board to "Dump Pepsi"

Activists to Pour Pepsi into Sewer Prior to Denver School Board Meeting on Thursday, February 6

Claiming that selling Pepsi in schools threatens children's health, activists will dramatically illustrate Thursday what the Denver School Board should do about sales of soft drinks in Denver schools: Dump Pepsi.

Prior to the School Board's February meeting, activists will dump the unhealthy beverage where in belongs—in the sewer.

The protest will take place Thursday, February 6, at 4:30 p.m. in front of the DPS administration building, 900 Grant Street.

"Our kids are far better off with Pepsi going down the sewer pipes than going down their throats," says Dr. Manny Salzman, who is leading the campaign against renewing the Pepsi contract. "If the School Board wants more overweight, diabetic kids with high blood pressure, it should allow Pepsi sales in our schools. Let's be clear: This is a public health issue."

The DPS' exclusive contract allowing Pepsi products to be sold in Denver schools is up for re-negotiation this year.

Fifteen percent of kids are overweight, up from 5% in 1980. Junk foods, including soft drinks, contribute to making children overweight. Overweight children are more susceptible to diabetes—the 6th leading cause of death in the U.S. Diabetic children are susceptible to high blood pressure and heart and kidney problems.

"Children are encouraged to buy soft drinks by accessible vending machines and by implied endorsement of soft drinks by school boards," adds Salzman.

Activists are encouraging citizens to offer their comments on the Pepsi contract at a School Board hearing Thurs., Feb. 6, at 7 p.m. The hearing follows the School Board meeting, which starts at 5 p.m. To speak at the hearing, citizens must call the school board at 303-764-3210. Organizers, who have formed "Citizens Against Pepsi," expect kids, teachers, parents, and grandparents of DPS kids—as well as concerned citizens—to attend their protest.

"The ad-hoc organization, Citizens Against Pepsi, was quickly formed by activists to promote a demonstration. About twenty protesters attended this event, which was covered by the local TV and print media. Local news media seek strong visual imagery."
CREDIT: JASON SALZMAN

TⱧE DⁱRTY DOZEN
LEAGUE OF CONSERVATION VOTERS ACTION FUND

FOR IMMEDIATE RELEASE
June 20, 2002

CONTACT: Dan Vicuña
(202) 454-4678
Andy Schultheiss
(303) 541-0362
lcvpress@lcv.org

LCV Targets Wayne Allard for DᵢRTY DOZEN Defeat
Allard AWOL on votes to protect Colorado's environment

DENVER, CO – Today the League of Conservation Voters (LCV) Action Fund launched a DᵢRTY DOZEN campaign to defeat Wayne Allard's bid for another six years of failing to protect the interests of Colorado families in a clean and healthy environment. Allard made the wrong choice for Colorado's air, water, and open spaces in 127 of the 139 career votes recorded on LCV's *National Environmental Scorecard*, including four straight years of scoring 0%, from 1997 through 2000. LCV punctuated its announcement with the release of a "Dirty 30" list of Allard's worst environmental votes. LCV expects to invest hundreds of thousands of dollars in its effort to inform Colorado voters that they deserve better than a Senator who will not stand up for their natural resources when it counts.

"Wayne Allard was an easy choice for LCV's Dirty Dozen because his 12-year voting record adds up to a giant step in the wrong direction for Colorado's environment," said Deb Callahan, LCV president. "When it was time to stand up for our natural resources, Wayne Allard was AWOL for Colorado."

Wayne Allard has worked hard to create the impression that he cares about Colorado's environment but his record clearly shows otherwise. He has touted a list of environmental achievements that he calls the "Clean 14" but many were of minor significance or were mainly the work of others. Allard's real voting record is better represented by the "Dirty 30," which includes his votes to let taxpayers rather than polluters pay the bill for cleaning up toxic waste sites, against fire protection funding, against renewable energy, against funding for land conservation, and for mine waste dumping on public lands.

LCV Action Fund's DᵢRTY DOZEN campaigns have targeted America's most anti-environmental congressional candidates for defeat since 1996. LCV's members have invested almost $8 million to defeat 23 of the DᵢRTY DOZEN's 37 targets. In 2000, LCV defeated candidates – including U.S. Sens. Spencer Abraham and Slade Gorton – who averaged a score of 10% the LCV *Scorecard*, while their successors averaged 93% in 2001. South Dakota's John Thune and Georgia's Saxby Chambliss are the other announced DᵢRTY DOZEN campaigns of the 2002 cycle. For more information visit www.lcv.org/campaigns/dozen.

- 30 -

Catchy labels like "Dirty Dozen" capture the news media's attention—especially when they are backed up with a substantive analysis, as explained with refreshing brevity in this news release.
CREDIT: LEAGUE OF CONSERVATION VOTERS

News Advisories

If you have information that you want to keep secret until a news event, send out a news advisory stating where and when the news event will be and what the topic is. For example, you may be releasing a report or announcing a lawsuit. Or a news advisory can serve as a "calendar listing."

A news advisory is written just like a regular news release with the appropriate date, phone numbers, and contact people. Following is a sample.

 **Planned Parenthood®**
of the Rocky Mountains

The mission of Planned Parenthood of the Rocky Mountains is to improve the quality of life by enabling all people voluntarily to exercise individual choice in their own fertility and reproductive health.

MEDIA ADVISORY   CONTACT:
June 6, 1997   Kate Reinisch: 321-PLAN (7526)

**Planned Parenthood Honors Graduates of
Their Teen Pregnancy Prevention Programs**
Community Leaders and Sports Stars Celebrate
High-Risk Teens Who Beat The Odds

What: Reception and Graduation Ceremony for *Dollar-A-Day*
            and *Male Achievement Network* Graduates

When: **Tuesday, June 10, 1997**
            Event: 5:30 to 7:00 PM
            Media Availability with Teens: 5:00 to 5:30 PM

Where: The Governor's Mansion, 400 E. Eighth Ave., Denver

Speakers: (Letter of support from Jane Fonda and Ted Turner will be read)
            Dani Newsum, KHOW Radio
            Lark Birdsong and Missy Masley, Colorado Xplosion
            Mark Knudsen, Colorado Rockies
            Graduates of PPRM's Teen Pregnancy Prevention Programs

Agenda: 5:00 PM   Media availability
            5:30 PM   Event begins
            6:00 PM   Ceremony begins
            6:30 PM   Ceremony ends
            7:00 PM   Event ends

Dollar A Day: An innovative teen pregnancy program which utilizes
mentoring, professional counselors, education, peer support and a token
monetary incentive to empower at-risk young women to delay pregnancy.
PPRM has 7 *Dollar A Day* groups with a 94% success rate.

Male Achievement Network (MAN): The intent of *MAN* is to encourage
young men to make responsible life choices regarding their sexuality and
involvement in teen pregnancy. *MAN* groups meet at 7 high schools and
provide participants with role models, support, information and education.

###

950 Broadway, Denver, Colorado 80203-2779 • 303-321-PLAN • FAX 303-861-0268 • Clinic Appointment 1-800-230-PLAN • Facts of Life Line (303) 832-5995

A news advisory contains even fewer details than a news release.
CREDIT: PLANNED PARENTHOOD OF THE ROCKY MOUNTAINS

Video for TV

If you're releasing a story and you've got "background footage" to go with it, state on your news release that video is available. Such videotape, called "B-roll," can give your story the video appeal it needs to make television news. Home video is widely used in newscasts, especially on local TV news. If you've got a dramatic home video, you can turn it into a story all by itself.

"It always helps to advance a story if there is home video that goes along with it," says Tom Donahue, Miami bureau chief for CBS News. "Quite often, we'll buy it." (See discussion of video news releases in the next chapter.)

Photos

If you have photos of the visuals that you plan to unveil at a news event, paste them into an e-mail so reporters know what's coming. Small papers will often use photos that you provide. (See Chapter 34, "Hit the Small-Time: Neighborhood and Rural News.")

Chotchkas

Avoid trying to catch the attention of journalists by giving reporters a gift or unnecessary trinkets. But some reporters enjoy this stuff—like a news release written on a cookie or a clever hat. If you give stuff away to journalists, make sure it's not too expensive and is truly creative or useful.

Embargoes

If you "embargo" a news release, you are—in theory—prohibiting journalists from using your information until some future date. For example, if you are distributing a document to reporters on May 3 and do not want any coverage until May 7, you would type "Embargo until 9 A.M. MST May 7" on the top of the release. You'd expect your story, if it were newsworthy, to appear on Web sites and on television and radio on May 7 and in morning papers on May 8. News services such as AP would distribute

it on May 7. (If you're distributing your release nationally, make sure you include a time zone, like EST, by your time.)
You should avoid placing an embargo on a news release. Here's why:

- News media commonly break embargoes or find a way to get around them.
- Advance coverage of an event usually leads to more coverage, not less.
- Generally, you should take coverage when you can get it. Tomorrow the sky may fall or a plane may crash, and you could get no coverage at all. (As an alternative to an embargo, you can let trusted journalists know that you've got an important story coming on a specific date.)
- Reporters may not take kindly to an embargo. "Most of the time, it's arrogant for a special interest group to embargo," says Mark Obmascik, an investigative journalist at the *Denver Post*.

One type of release, however, may merit an embargo. If you're releasing a lengthy report, you should consider giving reporters a couple of extra days to study it and perhaps get some reactions to it.

If you do embargo a release, do not distribute it widely. It should be sent only to reporters you know. Unless you have an ongoing relationship with a reporter, you're taking a substantial risk by giving him or her your breaking-news story before the release date.

I've repeatedly seen reporters break embargoes. Once, I explicitly told a well-known columnist at *USA Today* not to publish information about a report before the release date printed clearly on our news release. I opened up *USA Today* the next morning—one day before our release date—and there was a short piece about our report buried deep in the paper.

Another time, I helped line up four reporters, including one from the *New York Times*, who were interested in writing a story about a report I was releasing. My organization sent the report with an embargo request to each of them, including a reporter from the Associated Press, in advance. The AP reporter received our report and broke the embargo, publishing it a day before the release date. This resulted in the *Times* deciding not to cover our story. Fortunately, however, the AP put our story on the national wire and it was distributed to media outlets across the country.

15

Distributing a
News Release

ONCE YOU'VE GOT A MEDIA LIST, getting your news release out should be easy. You can e-mail or fax a release to an entire list of reporters with the push of a button. Just be sure to send your release to a specific journalist at each outlet—so you can place a follow-up call later to make sure it was received. (See Chapter 17, "It's the Follow-up Call, Stupid.")

How Should You
Deliver Your News Release?

Find out how journalists want to receive news releases and other information. Most reporters, especially at print outlets, like e-mail best, but fax is still preferred by many radio and TV journalists, especially those at local TV news outlets.

"Different editors have different preferences [e-mail, fax, or mail]; most important is that we get the information with a phone number," says Anne Henderson, deputy metro editor at the *Omaha World-Herald*.

By E-Mail

Most journalists like to receive news releases via e-mail, especially print journalists. Be sure to write an eye-popping subject line, and to list all recipients in the "blind carbon copy" or Bcc field.

116

Personalize as many e-mails as possible, and paste your news release (possibly with photos and links) into the e-mail—rather than attaching a file to the e-mail message.

Fearing viruses, lots of journalists don't open attachments. "No attachments," says Rob Eley, senior editor at the *Burlington Free Press*. "Most papers won't even open e-mails with attachments because of viruses."

"E-mail's best," says Keith Rogers, a reporter for the *Las Vegas Review-Journal*. "If I'm not interested, I can hit the clear button and it's gone. . . . I've covered entire stories through e-mail—sending questions and getting answers back. It's easier to e-mail than pick up the phone and call."

To compile an e-mail list, ask journalists for their e-mail addresses. The Websites of news outlets often list the e-mail addresses of staff, and media directories sometimes include e-mail addresses, but many reporters have a private address that works much better. In a pinch, you can even try looking up a journalist's e-mail address on a Website like www.people.yahoo.com.

By Fax

Many reporters want to receive news releases by fax. Journalists at local TV news outlets like to have a piece of paper that can be handed to a photographer or reporter who's assigned to cover an event. You can program most fax machine to send out dozens of news releases in succession.

Or you can hire a service to fax your news release simultaneously to hundreds of journalists. If you do, try to find a service that puts the recipient's name on a separate cover sheet. Also, different newspaper departments (features, editorial, sports) have different fax numbers. Make sure you've got the right one for the department you want.

By Mail

You will have trouble finding a journalist who prefers snail mail, but you can still use it. If you do, experiment with addressing the envelopes by hand—or send a postcard that need not be opened. As one newspaper editor told me, "If it's hand-addressed, you never know what it's going to be. If it is type-written or computer-generated, it can wait."

By Hand

Hand delivering your release to news outlets is unnecessary. In fact, you can't even get past the security desk at larger news organizations. So, unless your reporter comes down to greet you—which might annoy him or her—then you'll have to leave it with the guard.

By E-Mail Distribution Service

A growing number of companies distribute news releases by e-mail to hundreds of news outlets, regionally or nationally. For different fees, these companies might distribute your news release to college newspapers, op-ed editors, environmental reporters, political talk shows, and many other types of journalists or media outlets. You might try ascribe.org, which specializes in the nonprofit sector. The efficacy of these services varies, and even if you use them, you will have to create a list of targeted reporters and pitch them by phone. However, these services may score additional coverage for you. One benefit of the larger and pricier services (like U.S. Newswire and PR Newswire) is that their content is included in NexisLexis, a database of news stories that's popular among journalists and researchers.

By Satellite, Videotape, or Website

Some larger nonprofits spend big money hiring media consultants to send "video news releases" (VNR) to local TV stations and other broadcast outlets. This is a video version of a news release, with background footage and sound bites delivered by spokespeople. TV stations patch together a story with video from the VNR, which can be sent by mail or "streamed" onto a Website or distributed via satellite. Given the expense of VNRs and their at-best spotty use, especially by larger stations, they should be considered only in rare cases when you've got great visuals (possibly a controversial TV ad) and a highly newsworthy topic, preferably a breaking story.

You can try to identify Websites where you can post your news releases. For example, EurekAlert!, which has the backing of professional scientific societies, posts news releases for top science writers on its Website (www.eurekalert.org/). Also try ems.org.

When Should a Release Be Distributed?

For a news story, a news release should arrive at an outlet no earlier than a week before an event and no later than the day before. If you send it more than a week in advance, it will likely get lost. If you're promoting a feature story or an entertainment event like a concert, you should begin your outreach to feature writers at least three weeks in advance. (See Chapter 20, "Suggest Story Ideas to Journalists.")

How Many Reporters at a Single Outlet Should Receive the Release?

Generally, you should *not* simultaneously contact more than one journalist at a single news outlet. If a journalist at a large newspaper tells you that he or she will *not* cover your event, ask him or her who might cover it. Think creatively about pitches that might hook different types of reporters. Is there a business angle? Is there a celebrity? Would a particular columnist be interested in a human interest angle? You should not pitch a story to two reporters in the same department at the same time, for example, to two business reporters. But you can pitch them in succession. (See below for information on whom you should contact at different news outlets.)

"The biggest mistake groups make with the Associated Press is sending their news releases to too many people in the office," says David Briscoe at the Associated Press, echoing sentiments of other journalists. "All of us end up throwing them away."

Send Your Release to Daybooks

Each day at 5 or 6 A.M., the Associated Press sends its subscribers—which probably include all major news outlets in your area—a "daybook" listing news events scheduled to take place in the region on that day. Someone at most major news outlets reviews the daybook each morning. The daybook includes all kinds of news events. "We'll put almost anything on there, with the exception of entertainment events and anything of a money-making nature," says Bill Schiffmann, broadcast editor for AP's San Francisco bureau. A daybook for most cities typically contains five to ten items and may be updated to include breaking events during the day.

To have your event considered for the daybook, your news release should arrive at the AP by the morning of the day *before* your event. Address it to the "daybook editor." If appropriate, type "photo available" on the release. In some cities, different news services publish competing daybooks, for example, AP and Reuters in Washington, D.C. Make sure your event is listed in all of them. (For more information on the Associated Press and other news services, see the following section of this chapter and Chapter 32, "Promote a Story to Journalists at National News Outlets.")

Whom to Contact at News Outlets

Always contact journalists you know–or have been referred to— if you can. For information on how to develop contacts in the media, see Chapter 5, "Cultivate Relationships with Journalists."

If you don't have your own contacts, here is a description of the appropriate staff who should receive information about your event at each type of news outlet. (For more information on whom to contact at *national* news outlets, see Chapter 32, "Promote a Story to Journalists at National News Outlets.")

Daily Newspapers

Send your release to reporters or editors and photographers. If you don't have a specific name, "address it to the editor of the section of the paper that you think it would appear," advises Mike Tolson, senior editor at the *Houston Chronicle*. (Your media list should include names of reporters, photographers, news editors, calendar editors, editorial writers, columnists, and cartoonists.)

At larger newspapers, "beat" reporters make many of the news decisions—after checking with an editor. (Beat reporters cover issue areas, for example, education, environment, police.) If the paper is too small to have beat reporters, contact the city editor or editor. If your story does not relate to a particular beat, you should contact an editor unless you have a good relationship with a general assignment reporter. "If a reporter's too busy, he might toss [your story], but an editor might have another reporter available to cover it," says Jack Broom, a reporter for the *Seattle Times*.

You can help out the photo department—and your cause—by sending a release about your event directly to photo editors as well as to the appropriate reporter or news editor. At newspapers, unlike at television stations, reporters do not necessarily consider the visual aspects of a story to be all that important. As a result, reporters and editors often leave photographers in the dark, depriving them of the opportunity to shoot the exquisite visual prop you've created for your event.

"It's probably best to have us both clued into it," says *Boulder Daily Camera* photographer Cliff Grassmick. Address your release to the photo assignment editor or, at smaller papers, the photo editor. (See Chapter 26, "Influence Newspaper Photographers"; for information about how to contact columnists, editorial writers, calendar editors, and columnists, see Part Four, "How to Get News Coverage Without Staging a Media Event.")

Weekly or Monthly Publications

For monthlies, send your release to freelance journalists or reporters. At weeklies, you should call reporters or the editor. Most monthlies rely heavily on freelance journalists, making them your point of contact. (Freelance journalists sell their work on a piece-by-piece basis. They usually work for numerous news outlets, but most often they sell their work regularly to a handful of outlets.)

Remember that most weeklies and monthlies do not cover day-to-day events or breaking news, but they do cover many important issues in a more in-depth fashion. Don't ignore free weeklies just because they appear to be "alternative." Such publications are widely read by citizens and journalists alike. (See Chapter 34, "Hit the Small-Time: Neighborhood and Rural News.")

Local Television News

Send your news release to the assignment editor, unless you know a reporter. (At some stations, the planning editor should receive news releases.) As always, it's best to address a news release to a specific assignment editor.

Decisions about covering a day's events are usually made at a morning meeting of staff and reporters. Of course, a breaking story radically affects what dominates the limited news time on TV, just as it will alter the front page—but not all the pages—of a newspaper.

National Television News

Send your news release to a producer. It can be hard to get through to national network reporters and producers, but it could be worth it if you've got the time and the right story.

CNN has around-the-clock news programming and is often interested in timely events by citizens. Its audience is smaller than the network news programs but represents the public policy crowd (politicians, their staffs, concerned citizens, journalists), which you may want to reach. CNN is a fixture in many newspaper newsrooms around the world.

Don't forget other national cable and satellite news networks, particularly Fox and MSNBC, but also CNBC, and CNN International. Much of the programming on these cable outlets is dedicated to talk—much of it among screaming experts and much of it focused on the media frenzy of the day. Pitch your guest or topic to producers of a specific show that might bite, like *Hardball* on MSNBC or the *O'Reilly Factor* on the Fox Network. In addition to televising Congress, C-SPAN airs a talk show of its own and covers conferences, hearings, and lectures of national interest. The future will bring more cable news networks. (For more information on cable television, see Chapter 29, "Place Your TV Production or Information on Cable." For more information on whom to contact at national news outlets, see Chapter 32, "Promote a Story to Journalists National News Outlets.")

TV Public Affairs Programs, National TV Talk Shows, and TV News Magazines

Your best contacts are producers of specific shows you are targeting. These programs might plan shows on issues months in advance, and or they might want a guest for the hot news of the day. When you call, make sure you target a specific show (like *60 Minutes II*) and identify a producer by name.

News Radio

Send your news release to reporters or news directors. A typical media market might have only a couple of radio stations that have news departments with reporters. Make sure to try public radio stations, like National Public Radio affiliates, and community radio stations, which are often run mostly by volunteers.

Talk Radio and Pop Radio

Your best contacts are producers, hosts, or disc jockeys. For pop radio, contact the disc jockeys. For talk radio, contact the producer or host. (See Chapter 28, "Tune Your Cause to Talk Radio.")

News Services

Your best contacts are news editors and photographers. All kinds of news outlets, including newspapers, radio programs, and television stations, subscribe to news services that provide news stories, photos, video, and other information.

Of the news services, the Associated Press (AP) has the most offices across the United States, including scores of staff writers based in New York and Washington, D.C. Reuters (pronounced roy-ters) is the second largest news service. Bloomberg is the largest news service focusing on financial stories and information. Most, if not all, daily news outlets subscribe to AP and other news services.

At the state level, the Associated Press "news editor" who's on duty when your news release is received—or when you call—will decide whether your story merits AP coverage. You should contact "the news editor," not a specific person, unless you've got an established relationship. "In many cases, if we get something with a name on it, it winds up in a mail box," says Bill Schiffmann, broadcast editor for the AP's San Francisco bureau. "And if someone's on vacation, it may sit there for two weeks."

Unlike major local newspapers, most local AP bureaus don't have reporters assigned to beats or issue areas; they have generalists who cover the most important stories in the state. In Washington, D.C., New York, and other large cities, however, a handful of news editors—with reporters working for them—do cover beats such as foreign news and Capitol Hill. Thus, if you have a story that merits national coverage, you could try contacting the news editor or reporter who's responsible for coverage of your issue. You might get referred back to the AP office in your area, but you can then say you were referred by the national office, which might help you get covered. (Check out a media directory, like *Bacon's*, for a comprehensive list of AP's beat reporters in Washington, D.C., and elsewhere.)

If your story is covered by AP, it's likely you'll never see a reporter. AP reporters often don't have time to leave the office—or they might distribute your story after it appears in your local newspaper. By agreement, AP can lift content from most dailies. AP reporters write short news stories—often of less than a few hundred words. (For more on AP, including tips on how to attract AP to your story, see Chapter 32, "Promote a Story to Journalists at National News Outlets.")

Other news services include Bloomberg Business News, which has a large network of offices covering business stories; States News Services, which offers Washington, D.C., news; Reuters, which is larger in Europe than in the United States, but is growing here; and United Press International, which has endured deep cuts but still clings to life. Certain national newspapers, such as the *New York Times, Los Angeles Times,* and *Washington Post,* also distribute news stories to papers that subscribe. That's why you might see *New York Times* stories in your local paper. Some newspaper chains, for example, Gannett News Service, Hearst News Service, Knight-Ridder Newspapers, and Thomson Newspapers, maintain offices in Washington, D.C., and send stories to their networks around the country. There are numerous specialty news services as well, including AlterNet in San Francisco, serving alternative news media; Baptist News Service, serving state Baptist weeklies; Hispanic Link News Service, serving Hispanic-oriented weeklies; and many others. News services such as Creators Syndicate, King Features, and Universal Press Syndicate distribute the work of columnists, editorial cartoonists, and feature writers.

Some larger cities have their own local news services—for example, City News Bureau in Chicago—that cover local news and have local subscribers. There are also news services in foreign countries, such as Jiji Press in Japan or Agence France-Presse in France. If your story has international relevance, check for news services in the countries where you want to receive coverage. Some have offices in the United States.

Web-Based News Outlets

Send your news release to reporters or editors. But understand that there are few Web-based news outlets at the local level, and a relatively small number at the national level. Most of the news that you find on the Internet is generated by reporters who work for traditional print and broadcast news outlets. Their stories, plus those of wire services, provide most of the content for news sites on the Web. (See Chapter 35, "News on the Web.")

Use Diverse Media to Your Advantage

One key to publicizing a cause is to take advantage of the diversity of the media. Although the most powerful news media can be very similar (witness network television news), there are other outlets that specifically seek stories that the major media ignore or that serve specific audiences whom you may want to reach. And some small outlets may cater exactly to your target audience. For example, to communicate to a state legislator, you may seek coverage in a neighborhood weekly newspaper rather than a large metropolitan daily.

The fact that fewer people read the newspaper or listen to the radio does not mean you should focus your efforts on TV. The segment of the population that reads the paper may be exactly the one your campaign needs to reach.

16

Interviews

Y OU SHOULD PREPARE THOROUGHLY for any interview with a
reporter. This means not only knowing the facts about your issues but also how to translate these facts into language that's understandable to your audience. (Also see Chapter 3, "Strategic
Media Plans.")

Stay on Message

If you only read one paragraph in this chapter, choose this one:
The whole point of being interviewed is to communicate a specific message to your audience. Don't blow it by blabbing about
stuff that's not central to your message. Before any interview, be
clear on two or three points that you want to make—and touch
on them repeatedly during the interview.

For example, if your goal in an interview was to deliver the
"message" that local TV news airs too much mayhem, especially
crime, you could be prepared with these three points: (1) murder
is usually the lead story on local TV news; (2) crime rates are going down but crime coverage is increasing on local TV news; and
(3) local TV news stations dedicate more time to crime coverage
than any other topic.

In your conversation with a reporter, you would find opportunities to "bridge" an answer containing your message to the
questions asked. In other words, you would work your message
into your reply. For example:

Question: Is your dog named Spot?

Answer: Even my dog Spot knows that it's bad journalism to blow crime out of proportion by airing too many crime stories.

Question: Don't you think TV stations air crime stories because that's what people want?

Answer: People want balanced news, not crime every day as the lead topic for most TV news programs.

Question: So, you think *you* should decide what's news?

Answer: Why do journalists, who have the job and responsibility to decide what's newsworthy, dedicate more time to crime than any other topic—every day, even when crime rates are falling?

Question: Are you going to eat rice for dinner?

Answer: Sometimes I'm so sick after watching all the crime on TV news—even though crime rates are falling—that I'm not able to eat anything for dinner.

Question: You look like the type who enjoys aphrodisiacs?

Answer: I *would* enjoy seeing a balance of stories on local TV news, not just crime, crime, and mayhem—topped with a dose of fluff.

You get my point. Even the most absurd questions can be answered "on message." For help, call my mother-in-law, who always seems to steer a conversation back to her agenda.

Create Sound Bites

A sound bite is the type of speech commonly found on television and radio broadcasts. It is defined by how long it takes to deliver (five to twelve seconds) and by the style of language it contains.

Often, the most quotable sound bites are connected to the actual imagery of your event. For example, a nuclear reactor in Texas had a long history of deficiencies and was widely regarded as a "lemon." To protest the restart of this plant, activists dressed as lemons and used this sound bite: "Restarting this reactor would sour the economy of Texas."

Similarly, activists in New Mexico donned Pinocchio noses to illustrate their point that the governor of New Mexico was stretching the truth about the safety of a waste dump. The sound bite they chose: "The truth about the governor's position is as plain as the nose on my face."

If you're in a rush and need to create a good sound bite, start it with the phrase "I'm here today to . . ." If you want to highlight your organization, start the same phrase with your organization's name. Following are more sample sound bites.

- "The Pentagon budget should be used to defend America, not to line the pockets of defense contractors and special interests."
- "My yard is contaminated. Where are my kids going to play?"
- "Recycle America should change its name to 'Dump on China,' because it isn't recycling plastic; it's dumping it on China."
- "If the Norwegian government is unwilling to stop the whale hunt, we'll make them stop."
- "This law has nothing to do with medicine and everything to do with politics."

It's easy to complain about our TV culture, in which complex ideas must be reduced to sound bites to land in the news. But there's a reason for it. This type of communication reaches the widest audience. In other words, it works. People understand 10-second sound bites, and they've come to expect this style of communication in all aspects of public life.

Unfortunately, many nonprofits are stuck in mission-statement culture, which is the opposite of sound-bite culture. Nonprofit staffers talk about what they do as if they are reading mission statements, replete with jargon and multisyllabic words that make you want to run away from the person uttering them.

Anticipate Interview Questions

You should try to predict the questions you'll be asked in an interview. What are the typical arguments against your position? What problems has your organization faced? Look over recent articles about your issue and note the types of questions asked.

You also need to have answers ready about your funding and history.

Following are some typical questions asked by interviewers.

Why are you out here today?
Why are you releasing this report?
What's the point of this protest?
Do you really think this will have an impact?
Isn't this just a publicity stunt?
What's next?
Who's funding your organization?
How long have you been in existence?
Are you just an idealist?

Practice Your Answers and Sound Bites

The most visible spokespeople—including the president of the United States—practice prior to interviews. You won't regret practicing your answers and sound bites. Assign someone to ask you the questions you think a journalist might ask. Remember that journalists are busy and frequently fall back on stock questions, which leave you lots of room to say what you want.

Avoid Talking to a Journalist "Off the Record"

Sometimes, a "source"—like you—will speak to a journalist only under specific conditions. For example, a source might offer information to a reporter but not want his or her name associated with it. (Sometimes this is called "on background.") Or a source might not want his or her quote—or any information relayed during a conversation—used at all. (Sometimes this is called "off the record.")

The trouble is, journalists interpret terms like "off the record" differently. For example, if you are the spokesperson for a human rights organization and you are speaking "on background" or "not for attribution," does that mean your anonymous quote cannot be attributed to an "unnamed human rights group" or to the "human rights community" or to an "activist"?

Speak to journalists "on the record." There is usually no need for a spokesperson for a nonprofit organization to operate any other way. This means everything you say can be attributed to you, even something as casual as "Let me take off my rumpled jacket for this photo." Steve Trombulak of Middlebury College once told a reporter his personal opinion of logging-company executives. Only later did he realize his expletives might end up in print. To his dismay, they did.

Furthermore, your willingness to speak on the record attracts journalists: "[Nonprofit groups] are willing to say on the record what others aren't willing to say," says Tom Lippman, a former reporter for the *Washington Post*.

If you must place conditions on your conversation with journalists—and you have clear strategic reasons for doing so—don't use vague terms such as "off the record." Instead, explain to each journalist the specific conditions under which your information can be used. If you decide that only part of a long conversation should *not* be on the record, make sure you make it very clear when you are talking on the record and when you are not.

Tips for Any Interview

No matter what type of interview you are anticipating, certain fundamentals apply:

- Before your interview, ask about the topic and format. You could even ask what some of the questions will be. In addition, watch or read the publication or program, and find out as much as you can about the journalist who will interview you.
- Before the interview, e-mail or fax the reporter background information.
- An interview is never over even if the tape stops rolling.
- Everything you say to a journalist should be considered on the record.
- Be courteous to all media people, including camera operators and support staff.
- Never assume journalists are on your side even though they will often act as if they are.
- You should feel free to make a statement, then answer the question (for example, "I'll answer that, but first, by way of background, I want to say . . . ").

- Eliminate insider jargon and acronyms specific to your area of expertise.
- Never say "no comment." If you cannot talk about a subject, explain why.
- Keep your answers short, drawing on your message, sound bites, and anecdotes practiced.
- Don't address the reporter by name constantly. It sounds stilted.
- You can use either a reporter's first or last name depending on your style.
- Journalists like anecdotes.
- You don't have to answer hypothetical questions. If a question is speculative, say so and add that you'll answer it if the hypothetical situation becomes reality.
- There is not one type of "media personality." Be yourself.
- Even the most experienced spokespeople are nervous during interviews. Get used to the feeling and realize that your nervous energy can help you be more lucid.
- Tell a reporter what you think is the most important angle for him or her to write about.
- Humor is great if it's not cutesy. (Many journalists are, understandably, quite cynical and therefore relate to cynical humor.)
- Suggest questions that reporters should ask your opponents.
- It may also be appropriate to suggest questions journalists should ask *you.*
- If you need more time to think, ask the reporter to repeat the question or ask a clarifying question—or simply pause and think before answering.
- If you don't know the answer to a question, say so. Track down the answer later and call the reporter.
- Tell a reporter you have more to add if he or she overlooks something you think is important.
- Dress the way you want to appear. But remember your goal and audience. It's a shame when casual or ragged clothes distract your audience from what you are saying.
- Get to know the reporters in your community so that you can present information in language that meshes with their particular style, making it more likely that you'll be quoted.

Respect the professional relationship you have with reporters.

Tips for TV Interviews

- Determine the format. Will your interview be taped and edited later, like many local TV news interviews? Will it be live, like most cable talk shows? Or will it be live on tape, like many public affairs programs and some TV talk shows?
- TV interviews can be conducted either on location or in a TV studio with or without a reporter present. Live interviews can be more stressful, but look at them as an opportunity to send an unedited message to your audience.
- If you're staging an event, your TV interviews will probably be conducted at the site of your event with or without a reporter. If a reporter accompanies the camera operator to your event, it's more likely your event will appear on the news. (Sometimes the camera operator and the reporter are the same person.)
- I advise people, overall, to dress conservatively for television—to avoid alienating the audience with their clothes. (Any color is OK, if the style is appropriate.)
- Think about whether your jewelry (for example, a nose ring) will make people disregard what you say. Flashy earrings will be even more flashy if the TV camera zooms in on your face.
- Hats with a brim may cast a shadow across your face. Avoid them.
- Operating under the assumption that "a little tan never hurts your appearance," accept makeup if offered to you prior to an interview, and bring some if you need it. But if you look in the mirror and see that your makeup job looks bad (for example, clownlike), for goodness' sake get it off before you go on the air!
- Perspiration can be a problem, especially for bald people. If it's a big problem for you, you should consider applying powder before your interview and possibly during commercials. You can bring your own powder to your interview site.

- Bring a copy of your report or book for a close-up shot.
- Warm up your voice by talking for a few minutes before your interview.
- Breathe deeply before the interview.
- Speak slowly in five- to twelve-second sentences.
- Use action verbs in the present tense. Be forceful.
- Relax your shoulders and keep your body still.
- Don't lean forward or sway from side to side. Too much movement of any kind looks odd on TV. However, don't be stiff as a board, either.
- Make hand gestures or hold a prop.
- If you are standing at a podium, don't lean forward. The camera operators adjust the microphones to pick up your voice while you are standing up straight.
- TV reporters usually want you to look at them or the camera operator—not directly into the camera. If you are conversing from the field with the anchor back at the studio, you will want to look into the camera. (Ask the camera operator or reporter where to look if you are unsure.)
- Give brief answers to questions. The more tape they've got, the less control *you've* got over what gets on the air.
- Time zooms by when you're on TV. Get your highest-priority points out as soon as possible.
- If you're being taped and you think you've screwed up a sound bite, stop and repeat it. If you stutter or mispronounce a word, apologize and start again.
- If you're live on camera and the reporter is harassing you or a crowd around you is causing confusion, you can look into the camera and say something directly to the audience. This can be effective, but it should be used rarely because it can look canned and annoy the reporter at the site. (Once a police officer was being interviewed about whether a murderer would be caught. He looked directly into the live TV cameras and told the murderer out there that he would, indeed, be caught. This attempt at drama looked silly.)
- Interpret questions very broadly or, if necessary, ignore them completely and say what you want. This especially applies to TV interviews, in which many reporters will only take a sound bite and be on their way.

- Raise and lower your voice to make a point.
- Don't read a prepared statement.
- Deliver a sound bite in the form of a question. This is an excellent way to frame an issue and prompt a response from your opponents (for example, "Can they prove that the factory is safe?").
- Give examples that are as personal as possible. TV reporters are looking for emotion. Refer to concrete images.
- If necessary, ask to add a final comment to a taped interview.
- Expect, at the end of some taped interviews, a camera operator to shoot "cutaway" shots of you and the reporter talking. Often the back of your head will be photographed—or possibly the reporter asking questions. This footage can be inserted in the final story for editing purposes.
- Some TV stations have "beat" reporters who cover issue areas. You should recognize these reporters and be prepared for more detailed questions from them than you get from your average TV reporter.
- If you've got video footage that's relevant to the interview topic, offer it to the producer or reporter. Stations will sometimes use this "B-roll" footage for background shots.

Tips for Radio Interviews

Radio news interviews are much like those for television news, except, of course, they require good audio instead of video. Thus many of the tips for television interviews apply to radio with the following caveats:

- Warm up your voice prior to the interview by singing or yelling at your dog. (See Chapter 28, "Tune Your Cause to Talk Radio," for more tips on what to do before you go on the air.)
- Don't worry about speaking slowly on the radio as long as you speak clearly.
- Try to provide other sounds—besides voice—for radio (for example, chants, cheers, clapping, relevant music).

- A story on public radio may include a twenty- to thirty-second quotation. But you will seldom hear a sound bite of more than ten or fifteen seconds on commercial radio.
- The majority of radio interviews, like print interviews, are conducted by phone. Make sure your phone is in a quiet place, and—if you're live on the air—do not listen to the radio while you're being interviewed. There is a delay and it will confuse you. The delay can also cause the screeching sound known as "feedback."
- Radio audiences are largest during rush hour. Try to get on the radio at this time.

Tips for Print Media Interviews

Newspaper reporters, who often cover "beats" (issue areas), are more likely to engage in a detailed discussion of your issue than most broadcast journalists. Generally, there is more space in a newspaper to explain the subtleties of an issue. As a result, print journalists will likely ask for more quantifiable information and be less satisfied with broad rhetorical statements from you.

Nonetheless, it makes sense to practice delivering sound bites to print reporters. "Reporters have their ears open for a phrase that's going to ring," says *Rocky Mountain News* reporter Bill Scanlon. "There is nothing wrong with practicing."

- Avoid wild rhetoric that's more suited for TV.
- Don't ignore questions. Newspaper reporters usually want more precise answers to their questions than do TV interviewers.
- Ask a reporter to read back a quote of yours only if absolutely necessary. Reserve this for extremely critical quotes.
- Sometimes a print journalist simply wants a response to some event over the phone. This type of story is called a "reaction piece." You can often predict when you will get such calls and have a statement ready to read, allowing you to deliver a precise quote. (See Chapter 20, "Suggest Ideas to Journalists.")

How to Conduct Yourself After an Interview

You should be courteous, but not gushing, to all media personnel. They will thank you, and you should return the thank-you and suggest they call if they need further information. One time a talk-radio host beat me up for a full hour—cut me off, attributed statements to me that I did not make. I thanked him at the end, saying that some hosts wouldn't ask guests with different views to be on their shows. He told me to announce the name and phone number of my organization on the air. Then he asked me to repeat it. Two free plugs.

Make sure to take time to watch tapes of the shows you're on and read clips with your quotes. You'll find ways to improve. (Plus, it's fun.)

17

It's the Follow-up
Call, Stupid

You could have the country's best event, the planet's best news release, the universe's most up-to-date media list, and be blessed in heaven—and all of it may not matter unless you make follow-up calls to make sure journalists know about your event.

E-mailing, faxing, or mailing a release to a reporter does not guarantee that he or she will see it. E-mail overload is routine. At some outlets, the faxes pile up in oblivion unless a journalist makes a special effort to retrieve one.

"Absolutely the best way is to call," says Michael Hirsh, an international correspondent for *Newsweek*.

"It's a lot easier to ignore a piece of paper than a phone call," says *Albuquerque Journal* reporter John Fleck.

"A follow-up call can make the difference in getting on the air," says Leonard Nelson, Web director for KNBR radio in San Francisco. "If you're persistent, you stand a better chance."

Few journalists have layers of secretaries. You can get through. Keep trying.

Never assume you don't need to call. Once, a rally I organized was covered in advance by a major metropolitan daily newspaper. Because the paper had already informed its readers the rally was happening, I figured that I didn't need to call to remind editors to send a reporter to the event. No reporter from the paper showed. The rally had slipped through the cracks. I should have called.

When to Place a Follow-up Call

- For *daily* news outlets, call two or three days before your event. Then gauge—depending on journalists' interest and your history with them—whether to call again the morning of *the day before* your event. (For information on which journalists to call, see Chapter 15, "Distributing a News Release.")
- For weeklies and monthlies, call as appropriate, depending on deadlines.
- Call all local television stations again *the morning of* your event.
- Call editors between 11 A.M. and 1 P.M. because they usually have morning meetings. Call reporters early in the day. "The worst time ever to call is when we're on deadline," says Keith Rogers, a reporter for the *Las Vegas Review-Journal*. "I've got a story that's got to get done, and the clock is ticking."
- If your stunt has good visuals, call the photography department of daily newspapers the day before your event.

Tips for an Effective Follow-up Call

- The day before your event, call the Associated Press "daybook editor" to make sure your event is listed in the daybook (For information on the AP daybook, see Chapter 15, "Distributing a News Release.")
- Don't trust voice mail. Reach a person—not a machine. But *do* pitch an answering machine if you've tried everything and time is running out. (You can call at night and talk to the night editor.)
- Identify yourself and ask if the release has been received.
- If it has not arrived, say you'll fax or e-mail a copy. Ask if the journalist has a minute to hear about the event on the phone. If so, make a thirty-second pitch about the event, which you should practice in advance (examples further on). "I don't have time to sit on the phone for twenty minutes and find out there's no story there," says Craig Maclaine at Radio Canada International.

- Call again to make sure your news release was received after you sent it a second time.
- If the journalist has received your release, ask if he or she has any questions. (Ask in a way that explains your event: "Do you have any questions about our 10 A.M. news conference tomorrow at the jail to announce our new initiative on violence prevention?")
- If you are making lots of long-distance follow-up calls—and your budget is tight—let the phone ring twice and hang up before the answering machine picks up. Most journalists answer the phone after the first ring if they're taking calls. Keep calling back until you get a person.
- Don't give up. Be persistent.
- Don't delegate follow-up calls to new volunteers or entry-level staff. This is a mistake because chances are the follow-up call will play a large role in determining whether a reporter covers your event. Also, phone calls offer you a chance to interact with journalists and develop credibility.

Four Sample Follow-up Calls

By the time you're making follow-up calls, you should already have identified a specific journalist to pitch your story to. (See Chapter 15, "Distributing a News Release," for tips on whom to contact.) And you should have addressed your release directly to him or her. (Never send a fax to, say, the *Baltimore Sun* without a name attached to it.) If you have not selected a specific journalist, your call will probably be routed to a student intern or possibly an editor. Your event may still be covered, but you're better off when you know whom you want to reach.

Sample Follow-up Call for a TV
Assignment Editor or TV Reporter

You: Hello, I'm calling from People for a Livable Downtown to make sure you received our news release about our plans to release giant balloons to show how ugly the

new skyscraper will look downtown. Five neighborhood
groups are opposing construction of the building.
Assignment Editor: Let me check. . . . I don't see it.
You: We're releasing the balloons tomorrow to dramatize
how massive the new skyscraper will be. I'll fax the release again right now.
Assignment Editor: Thank you.

At least half the time, reporters will not be able to locate your
news release when you call. You should fax or e-mail it again and
call again to make sure it was received the second time.

Another Sample Follow-up Call for a
TV Assignment Editor or TV Reporter

You: Hello, I'm calling from People for a Liveable Downtown to make sure you received our press release about
our balloon protest tomorrow at 10 A.M. in front of the
train station.
Assignment Editor: Hold on. . . . Yes, now I've got it.
You: We believe the proposed skyscraper would ruin the
character of the city for the loft-dwelling residents, and
we don't think people understand just how big the skyscraper will be. That's why we're going to tie the giant
balloons to a string and let them rise to the height of the
proposed building.
Assignment Editor: When will this take place?
You: Tomorrow, Wednesday, at 10 A.M. in front of the train
station downtown. A few neighborhood leaders will
speak; then we'll release the giant, colorful balloons.
Assignment Editor: We'll probably send someone down
there.
You: Thank you.

When you are pitching a story to a television journalist, remember that the substance of the story is of equal or lesser value than
the video possibilities. Always emphasize the visual components

of your story. If you don't have any, you'd better think of some if
you want TV coverage.

Sample Follow-up Call for a
Newspaper Editor or Reporter

> You: Hello, I'm calling from Rocky Mountain Media Watch
> to make sure you received our press release about our re-
> port documenting that crime coverage on local TV news
> is up while national crime rates are dropping.
>
> Reporter: Do you have something in writing?
>
> You: Yes, I just sent you an e-mail describing our report
> covering local TV news in 100 cities, including your city.
>
> Reporter: I'll look for it. When did you send it?
>
> You: I just e-mailed it.
>
> Reporter: Hold on a minute. . . . Yes, I've got it here.
>
> You: You'll notice that the number of murder stories on lo-
> cal TV news in your city doubled over the past year, but
> the murder rate is down in your area.
>
> Reporter: What group are you with?
>
> You: Rocky Mountain Media Watch has conducted annual
> studies of local TV news since 1994. Our reports have re-
> ceived national coverage in the past, and your predeces-
> sor covered our report last year.
>
> Reporter: I'm in the middle of something else right now.
> Where are you going to be in an hour?
>
> You: You can reach me at the phone number on the press re-
> lease all day.
>
> Reporter: Thank you.
>
> You: Would you like me to e-mail you the five-page execu-
> tive summary?
>
> Reporter: Yes. Do that.
>
> You: Thank you. I'm looking forward to speaking with you
> later.

Newspaper reporters are usually interested in stories with
new information from credible sources. In this case, the reporter
seems to be interested in the story. Otherwise, he would not have

asked where to reach you or requested the executive summary. In the previous example, it would make sense for you to call again in a couple of hours even if you do not receive a call first. You might say that you wanted to make sure that he received your second e-mail.

Another Sample Follow-up Call
for a Newspaper Reporter or Editor

> You: Hello, I'm calling from Rocky Mountain Media Watch to make sure you received our press release about our report documenting that crime coverage on local TV news is up while national crime rates are dropping.
>
> Reporter: Yes, I just received your e-mail.
>
> You: You'll note that your city had more stories about robberies on local TV news than any other city. Yet robberies are down in your area. Do you have any questions about our report?
>
> Reporter: No.
>
> You: Is this a story you or someone else there might be interested in?
>
> Reporter: We just ran a two-part series on the local anchors that touched on this.
>
> You: Yes, I saw that. It was an interesting piece—a fair and balanced treatment of the subject, I thought. But our report focuses more on the content of the news rather than on the personalities of the anchors. Maybe there's something different in our report.
>
> Reporter: I don't think so. We asked them about the crime coverage, and they justified it.
>
> You: Well, thank you for your time.
>
> Reporter: Let me know when your next report comes out.
>
> You: I sure will.

You have to be able to lose gracefully. It hurts in the short term, but it pays later because you leave the impression with the reporter that you are a reasonable professional whom she can call for information. You should gently try to persuade a reporter to cover your story, but you should not argue. "Not every news release groups fax us will get in the paper," says Jack Broom, a reporter at the *Seattle Times*. "They shouldn't give up."

Don't think journalists are doing you a favor by covering your event. Remember that journalists rely on sources like you to feed them story ideas and information. They need you as much as you need them.

18

News Conferences
and Media Kits

WHEN MANY CONCERNED CITIZENS and activists think of publicity, what pops into their minds is "news conference." In reality, a news conference is usually the wrong way to attract the media. It's a much better idea to stage an event that includes your spokespeople addressing a crowd or doing something. After the event, make a spokesperson or two available to give individual interviews as requested. (See Chapter 1, "Think Outside the Stratosphere.")

"Simply covering a news conference doesn't happen very often," says Cathy McFeaters, news director at KVUE-TV, Austin's ABC affiliate.

But news conferences may be the right approach if you expect many reporters to attend your event, and you want to make a statement to all of them at once.

If a news conference is called for, the appropriate timing and location would be the same as for other types of media events. (See Chapter 10, "The Best Times to Get Coverage" and Chapter 11, "Where to Stage a Media Event.")

Outdoor or Indoor News Conferences

Whenever possible, hold press conferences *outside* with backup arrangements for bad weather. You'll generate the best visual imagery this way. You don't have to worry about providing electricity for lights and camera equipment, but do consider camera angles and provide risers if you expect a major media frenzy.

News Conferences by Phone

An alternative to an in-the-flesh news conference is a news conference by phone. Here's how you do it. Distribute a news release inviting journalists to participate from the phone of their choosing. To do so, they must sign up in advance by e-mailing, calling, or faxing you. (See sample news release in Chapter 14, "News Releases.") You then set up a conference call with a conference call service, and give journalists who signed up for the call the dial-in number and the access code for the conference call. If you expect many reporters, you should ask them to e-mail questions during the conference call to a moderator, who will present the questions to the speakers. (This is an especially good option if you expect interest from reporters from around the country.)

News Conference on the Web or by Satellite

It's still expensive, but you can transmit video of a news conference live via the Internet. (Transmitting live video from a Website is called "Webcasting.") To do this, you hire a consulting company, which will 1) set up a Website for the Webcast, 2) establish a link to the new Website from your Website, 3) shoot digital video of your news conference, and 4) upload the video live to the Website for the viewing pleasure of your audience. (If you pay enough money, the video can be "studio quality," meaning it can be used on TV.) You would tell reporters about the upcoming Webcast in advance and ask them to register to gain access if they are interested. Reporters who log in can submit questions via e-mail to a moderator, who sorts through the e-mails as they are received and asks the questions of the participants. Reporters who missed the live event can log on to the Website later and watch "on-demand streaming" video of the event. ("On-demand streaming" is the term for video that can be accessed from a Website at any time.) If you don't have money for the live Webcast, you can go directly to on-demand video, for a fraction of the cost.

If you've got big bucks, another option is to broadcast a news conference via satellite, allowing TV newsrooms around the country to pick it up. Again, a consulting company sets up the satellite "live shoot" at your media event. You pitch broadcast news outlets, providing them with the satellite coordinates if they want to record the video. If desired, you can collect questions from reporters via e-mail. You can also buy satellite time to distribute a newsworthy TV advertisement or other video.

For highly targeted interviews, media consultants will set up a Satellite Media Tour (SMT). You schedule live interviews with broadcast journalists around the country. Sitting in a TV studio, your spokesperson conducts the interviews one at a time, live via satellite, answering questions from local journalists in different cities.

Tips for Staging a News Conference

- Practice the news conference in advance, including questions.
- Place your group's logo in front of the podium.
- Make sure your amplification system is adequate.
- Assign someone to greet reporters and to ask them to write their names on a "sign-in" sheet.
- Plan for a maximum of four speakers to make presentations of five minutes each.
- Put your most important speakers on first.
- Create props for your speakers to hold or point at, especially if they are the only visual element of your event.
- Speakers should dress in formal clothes unless they are in costumes or their clothes are somehow related to the message they are trying to send. (Many activists eschew dressing up, as if it were a litmus test of their sincerity. But why go to all the effort of trying to reach mainstream media and then distract or, worse, alienate your audience by wearing overly informal clothes?)
- Be aware that photographers frequently arrive at press conferences early to get a candid photo of participants doing something besides standing in front of a podium. Make

sure your candid shot is the one you want by preparing for photographers who come early.

- TV crews often shoot the news conference room. These shots look better if the majority of the seats are filled. Have supporters on hand to fill empty seats.
- If only a few reporters arrive on time, delay five minutes or longer to see if more show up. But if you've got a sizable group assembled—particularly TV cameras—get started on time. You can't predict when the next carjacking will send the TV cameras running off.
- A moderator should cut off speakers who run on too long.
- Allow ten minutes for questions.
- A news conference should seldom last longer than a half hour.
- Journalists who want more information can ask questions after the event.
- Do not restrict your press conference to journalists, but be prepared for disruptions (see further on).
- Food and beverages are not required, but non-alcoholic beverages are nice to offer.
- Plan to gather coverage (clips, video, and so on) of your event.
- E-mail, fax, or deliver your press kit to reporters who seemed interested, but did not show up.

Assemble a Media Kit

Easy-to-read information should be distributed to journalists at your event. If you have more than three pieces of paper, put them in a folder with your organization's logo on it. This is called a media packet or kit.

It's always tempting to make the mistake of giving a journalist too much written information. You will impress a journalist much more by demonstrating that you recognize his or her real needs.

Journalists obtain most of their information from conversations, not from written sources. Don't feed the recycling bins in the newsroom. Keep your press packets simple and slim. Following is a list of materials for a press packet.

- Your news release
- Brief biographies of speakers at your event
- A brochure or fact sheet about your organization
- A fact sheet or article about the issues you are addressing
- Key information relating to your event (summary of a report, copies of documentation)

Disruptions at a News Conference

Once I was in the middle of speaking at a news conference at the unveiling of a series of twelve billboards at the gates of the Rocky Flats nuclear-bomb plant near Denver. I must have been saying something right because suddenly a man from the audience started denouncing Greenpeace and me. He shouted, and the TV cameras started to swing toward him. We had about 100 people at the news conference, far outnumbering the protester.

Inspired by Allen Ginsberg's Buddhist chants at demonstrations, I initiated a chant among the audience. "Close Rocky Flats," we chanted, completely drowning out the single protester's cries and showing for the television cameras how small a minority he represented. He eventually quieted and we continued with our speeches.

This response to a disruption at a news conference worked well, but most often you won't have 100 supporters to help you chant. In general, the best way to deal with disruptions is to ignore them as long as possible and be polite and decent. If you can't ignore heckling or disruptions, apologize to reporters and ask the disruptive person to calm down or leave. If he or she refuses, threaten to call the police and continue with the news conference. If this is impossible, stop the news conference and offer to do individual interviews.

If you are asked obnoxious questions by "reporters" who may be your opponents, try to answer them and move on. If you suspect that people asking such questions are not really reporters, ask them to identify themselves and move on to other questions.

19

Assess

AFTER YOUR MEDIA EVENT OCCURS, take time to discuss how it went.

If you got coverage, can you generate letters to the editor from "ordinary" citizens, highlighting your message?

Don't take it personally if your event receives scant coverage. It wasn't your fault that Mayor Blunder broke his leg tripping over a pothole. Remember, about 60 percent of the newspaper can be ads, and only a third of most local TV news shows is "news," and most of this is crime coverage.

And many radio stations are closing their news departments completely and laying off reporters.

Still, if you are shut out of the news, consider complaining. (See Chapter 6, "How and When to Complain About Coverage.") But don't assume that you didn't get covered because you're on a blacklist of unacceptable subjects. Whereas the ownership interests of media corporations can influence news coverage, the factors—including editorial staff—that combine to determine what's news at mainstream outlets change daily. Don't read Noam Chomsky's ideas about self-censorship among journalists so closely that you end up giving up on the mainstream media. Chomsky himself wouldn't advocate this approach.

Yes, the news media are increasingly concentrated in the hands of a decreasing number of corporations. But this does not necessarily mean you'll be excluded no matter how unconventional your views are.

Don't quit. As Juliet Whitman of *Westword* put it: "It's hard for a paper to ignore people who just don't give up."

Don't quit. Ongoing communications efforts will change the long-term direction of our society. CREDIT: JASON SALZMAN

If you succeeded in generating coverage, analyze it closely and identify ways to improve next time. Make sure you maximize the benefit from media coverage about your event, as described in the next section.

Tips for Maximizing the
Benefit from News Coverage

- Even the most news-obsessed policy wonks don't see every article in the newspaper or watch TV twenty-four hours a day. Send all your "targets" (politicians, journalists, staff, executives, allies) digital and hard-copy versions of news coverage. This can create the illusion of a larger media event.
- E-mail clips to donors.
- Distribute media coverage within your own group.
- Post electronic clips on your Website.
- Extract quotes from articles—as politicians often do in election ads—to put in fact sheets, brochures, and other documents for the general public. A quote from a newspaper article, no matter how insignificant the article, gives you legitimacy in the eyes of many people.
- Use clips in press packets at future events.
- Use video of TV coverage in public outreach and on the Web.

Remember that eight fleeting inches of ink in the daily newspaper can be next to worthless if it is not linked to a strategy for winning your campaign (for example, reaching decisionmakers or a target audience).

Think strategy first, media second.

Part FOUR

How to Get News Coverage Without Staging a Media Event

CREATING A NEWS STORY THROUGH a media event, as described in Part Three of this book, is one way to draw attention to your cause. But there are many other ways to publicize your message in the news media.

You need to survey the options, each explained in a different chapter of this section, and select the ones that make strategic sense—based on your goals and target audiences. You may conclude that suggesting a story idea to a reporter, booking talk radio appearances, or publishing a guest opinion (op-ed column) is more useful than organizing a media event—and easier.

20

Suggest Story Ideas to Journalists

DAY AFTER DAY, REPORTERS ARE expected not only to write stories but to uncover them. They need your help. They want you to "pitch" them new information about an issue, and they want ideas about new ways to cover it. But they don't want to be pestered with irrelevant information or inane story ideas.

Your job is to know journalists and your issue well enough to give reporters what they need. Pitching story ideas over the phone or by e-mail should be a priority of any publicist. It usually requires little time and can have a powerful impact.

"You can reach almost any journalist in America just by calling," says Michael Hirsh, an international correspondent for *Newsweek*.

"I'm looking for background information and ideas for stories," says Lorenz Wolf-Doettinchem, a correspondent for *Stern*, a German weekly magazine similar to *Newsweek* and *Time*.

Tips for E-Mailing or Calling Journalists with Story Ideas

If you know a reporter, pitch him or her by e-mail. If not, you should make your pitch by phone—but have an e-mail ready to send as a follow-up. If you can't get through on the phone, try e-mail first.

- Track your issue carefully in the news and note which reporters and news outlets seem to be most receptive to your information. Try them first. *"Dateline NBC* will look for a more in-depth story, while *Nightly News* is news of the day," says Ed Litvak, an assignment editor for NBC News. "There are certain stories that work for a morning audience that won't work for the evening."
- Think constantly about story ideas and scour your own sources for new information. Realize that journalists don't have the time you do to think about the progression of your issue. Your goal should be to stay ahead of the media with story ideas. Paul Day, a reporter for Denver's KCNC-TV, a CBS affiliate, says: "It's always helpful to be thinking a half week in advance. I shouldn't be starting a day from scratch."
- Ask yourself if your information or idea is of significant interest. Often we become so buried in our issues that we mistake insignificant changes for newsworthy developments. "Some [organizations] have the attitude that their story is the only story in the world," says Craig Maclaine, a reporter for Radio Canada International.
- Try to find at least three examples that illustrate a *trend*. And suggest a story about this trend.
- Suggest some stories that don't involve you and in which you would not expect to be quoted. This adds to your credibility.
- Offer story ideas gently. "There's nothing a journalist likes less than being told what to write," says Michael Hirsh at *Newsweek*. "Instead, say, 'I found out something interesting about ABC corporation in Indonesia.'"
- Remember that journalists don't just want *information*; they want stories.
- Don't request a meeting. It's too time-consuming for journalists.
- Ask if a reporter has a minute to talk. If so, lay out your idea in less than a minute, referring to visual elements if you are talking to a television journalist.
- Practice your pitch in advance.

- Think of ideas to get journalists out of the office. Sometimes they welcome the chance to get away from the desk for a half-day. A media-savvy biologist I met takes journalists into the field with him on research projects.
- Be cognizant of how frequently you call a reporter. There is no rule about how often is too often because circumstances dictate different approaches. But don't overdo it.
- When you speak with a radio or TV journalist, remember that he or she is listening not only to what you say but to how you say it. You should look at your conversation as an audition for the show.
- When a journalist says, "I'm not interested," don't argue. Try again some other time with another idea. Most of the time, you get rejected. You just have to fail and move on to the next pitch—quickly.

Exclusive Pitches

You can pitch a story to more than one journalist at a time. But often it makes more sense to offer a journalist an "exclusive," meaning that you will not give your story to any other journalists. (If you do this, consider whether giving an exclusive to one reporter can make other reporters angry with you.) If you decide to speak to only one reporter, make sure he or she knows that you are offering an exclusive. Your chances of being covered are better.

It's perfectly legitimate to tell a reporter that you will offer him or her an exclusive but that you need to know within a day or two whether he or she plans to use the story.

Sample News Story Pitch by Phone

Reporter: This is Joanne Reporter.

You: Hi, Joanne. It's Jerry Button from Save the Fishies. If you have a minute, I thought I'd let you know about a development in the dead-sardines issue.

Reporter: Sure. Let's hear it.

You: You recall that sardines almost disappeared from the ocean around here in the 1990s. Congress enacted tough regulations. Well, the chief sardine weigher says more pounds of sardines have been caught this year than any year since 1992. The regulations, he says, seem to be working.

Reporter: You heard this from the chief sardine weigher?

You: Yes. I was at the dock and I stopped by the chief weigher's office.

Reporter: That's interesting. Who would've expected things to turn around so quickly?

You: That's what I thought. So I called Professor Fishhead. He told me that sardines are one of the fastest-reproducing fish on the planet. Given the chance, they do their thing quickly.

Reporter: Do you recall the name of the chief weigher you spoke with at the dock?

You: Yes. I've typed her name, a chronology, and other information for you. I'll e-mail it to you.

Reporter: That would be great. I'll give her a call, check in with Professor Fishhead and call you back. This looks like a good story.

You: Should I e-mail it to jreporter@newspaper.com?

Reporter: No, I prefer jscribe@aol.com. I check it more often.

You: Thanks. I won't talk to anybody else about it. When do you expect to work on this?

Reporter: I've got time on Monday. I'll get back to you by the middle of next week.

You: I'll look forward to hearing from you.

Sample News Story Pitch by E-Mail

From:	Jerry Button
To:	Joanne Reporter
Subject:	Area Sardines Booming Again

Dear Joanne:

You may recall that we met about six months ago at the reception for Sardinesville Mayor Rosa Cannery. I told you about our organization, Save the Fishies (www.savethe-fishies.org).

I've found some interesting information about the sardines in our area. The sardines almost disappeared around here in the 1990s. Congress subsequently enacted controversial regulations.

The chief sardine weigher, Francis Scale, told me yesterday that more pounds of sardines have been caught this year than any year since 1992. The regulations, he says, seem to be working.

I called Professor Fishhead at Sardinesville University. He told me that sardines are one of the fastest-reproducing fish on the planet. Given the chance, they do their thing quickly.

I've put together background information—including a chronology of developments relating to the sardine saga.

Please let me know if you are interested in this.

If I don't hear back from you by e-mail within two days, I will give you a call.

Sincerely,
Jerry Button
322–xxx–9873
www.savethefishies.org

Pitching Feature Stories

It can be more intimidating to pitch an idea for a feature story—a lengthy piece with human details and depth—than a news story, which is generally shorter with a factual focus.

"News" has some defining characteristics even if they're amorphous. But features are harder to define. After all, what's feature-worthy? In the hands of a good writer, anything can be a feature. Even my mother-in-law can be a subject for a feature story. So how does a feature writer decide what to cover in a world spilling over with potential feature articles?

The answer is this: Like other journalists, feature writers cover what they hear about or stumble across—or what their editors tell them to write about. If feature writers stumble across you (with your assistance), you can help them think of subjects for articles—just as you might help a news reporter think of news stories.

Feature writers are looking for good story ideas, and they want to hear from you, especially if your idea matches their interests.

"Do your research," says Colin Covert, a feature reporter for the *Star Tribune* in Minneapolis. "Tailor your story to the tastes of individual reporters."

Tips for Generating a Feature Story

- At a newspaper, feature stories are written both by news reporters and by designated feature writers. You can pitch feature ideas to both.
- Develop contacts with feature writers. (As with other media outreach, contacts help and should be cultivated, but they are not essential.)
- If your feature idea relates to an event, pitch it to feature reporters at least two weeks before the event.
- You don't need to write a news release to generate a feature. In fact, having one can turn some reporters off to your story idea.
- Have written information or background video ready. In some cases, a short e-mail or letter followed by a phone call can be productive, especially because it's hard to catch feature writers on the phone, and they may not return your phone calls.
- In pitching feature stories by phone, follow the professional protocol that you would with other journalists: Respect deadlines. Get right to the point. Practice your pitch.
- In many cases, you'll want to work exclusively with one journalist on a feature story. Use common sense to decide when exclusivity is necessary.
- You don't need to waste time saying your name unless you're known to the journalist. Say, "I'm calling from . . ." rather than "I'm Jane Button from . . . "
- With the right idea and the right visual punch, your feature might be useful for a TV news magazine, local TV news, or national news magazine. On local TV news, "soft news"—which could include your feature story—is one of the top subjects behind disaster and crime.

- When you are trying to persuade journalists to accept your feature topic, don't limit yourself to staff journalists. Freelance writers are also looking for good ideas. You should collect names of freelance journalists. Call the freelancers who work for a news outlet that might be appropriate for your feature story.

21

Hook Your Story to Breaking News

JUMP ON OPPORTUNITIES TO PUBLICIZE your *message* when your *issue* is already in the news. If Moses had given us the ten commandments of successful activist PR, this would be in the top five.

Why? Because when your issue is getting media attention, you don't need to convince journalists that it's newsworthy. Your issue is already news! You just need to offer them a story or photo opportunity that illustrates a new or local perspective, dramatizes a point of view, or advances the debate somehow.

Here's a simplistic explanation—straight from the mouth of a journalist—of why this works:

"News is what is really happening," says Krystian Orlinski, an editor for Reuters Television, a news service. "You have to deal with things that are right there on the top of the agenda."

If a major story has broken in the national news media about your cause—or there is an ongoing national debate about it—local and national news outlets may be looking for "local angles" about the story. Similarly, if a major story has broken in the local news media about your cause and the media have not heard from community groups—or even citizens representing a different perspective on a given issue—your story may be a hit.

But you've got to act fast—preferably no later than the day after the news breaks. The more time that elapses between the major news event and your response, the less coverage you can expect to receive.

Here are some examples:

- Activists held a quick news conference after the federal government halted all imports of Chilean fruit because cyanide was discovered on some Chilean grapes. At the news conference, the activists displayed a cigarette and a bushel of Chilean grapes. They explained that one cigarette had more cyanide than one bushel of grapes. Yet the federal government was not acting to stop people from smoking cigarettes.

- After three kids got hit by cars on their way to school, Denver Mayor Wellington Webb put on a safety vest and led school children through the crosswalks to school, promoting volunteerism—and scoring big coverage.

- Planned Parenthood activists knew that TV reporters would be looking for a "local reaction" to the state of the union address, in which the president was going to make a controversial statement about abortion. The activists offered the reporters an image, inviting them to one of their homes while they watched the speech. It worked. The activists were pictured on TV reacting positively to the president's statements about abortion rights.

- After contestants on the TV show *Survivor* barbecued rats, eight PETA activists—including one in a rat suit—managed to make national news by protesting the killing of the rodents.

- Planned Parenthood held a candlelight vigil after a doctor was shot by anti-abortionists. It was front-page news because it was staged the day after he was shot—not the next week. (Vigils with photogenic candles get attention.)

Stunts (like the PETA example) hooked to news stories can be most effective for television. This is because television news often derives its newsworthiness from imagery, not necessarily from the importance of any information. Television journalists, with their thirst for images, may organize an entire story around one photogenic stunt.

Following are some "news hooks" that can carry your story into the media:

A public hearing
A court decision
The passage of a bill
A shooting at a school
A fire started by a camper
A veto
A major speech
The release of a report about teen depression
A holiday
A nomination
A high-profile rape
A celebrity arrested for child abuse
The one-year anniversary of a major shooting

Worm Your Way into the News

The most brilliant publicists figure out creative ways to worm their issue into a news story that's getting lots of attention, *even if the news story is not ostensibly about their issue.* Recall my earlier story of how PETA activists sent a letter to convicted bomber Timothy McVeigh requesting that he eat a vegetarian meal as his last supper before being executed. Most people would think that an execution of a murderer has nothing to do with vegetarianism. But PETA found relevancy out of apparent irrelevancy and made national news.

Giant corporations are good at finding ways to connect their products to big news frenzies. For example, Taco Bell floated a giant target in the Pacific Ocean for the returning Mir space station to hit. If it hit the target, free tacos for everyone. It missed, of course, but the stunt was covered by two national morning TV talk shows.

If you choose, you can offer quotes to journalists—or the opportunity to be interviewed—when a major story breaks. Journalists are looking for comments from interest groups.

Tips on Offering Quotes to Journalists in Response to Breaking News

- Monitor CNN or news radio so you can hear about breaking news at about the same time print reporters do, allowing you to prepare quotes for the stories they are writing for the next morning's papers.

- Only react to breaking news that is clearly significant.
- Contact news reporters who you know cover day-to-day breaking news.
- If you call reporters, prepare your reaction quotes in advance and practice delivering them.
- If you fax or e-mail your reaction to reporters, keep the news release to about a half-page with a good headline and two quotes. (See Chapter 14, "News Releases.")
- Follow up any news release with a phone call. (See Chapter 17, "It's the Follow-up Call, Stupid.")
- Don't delay. You should get your reaction out the door as soon as you hear about the story, ideally before it hits the newspapers.
- If you work on a national issue, consider organizing a phone briefing linking national journalists with your experts from across the country (See Chapter 18, "News Conferences and Media Kits," and the next chapter.)

Put two activists together and instead of *doing* something, they'll form two committees. While the committees are meeting, opportunities for coverage are lost and the cause suffers. You have to speak to the media when they are available.

22

Influence Editorial Writers and Other Journalists

THE OFFICIAL POSITIONS OF A newspaper are found in its editorials, which are unsigned opinions usually printed beneath the paper's name and vital statistics—the editor's name, the publisher's name, and so on. (These are *not* the signed opinion pieces in the paper by local and national pundits. For information on influencing these opinion columnists, see Chapter 25, "Persuade a Columnist to Write About Your Issue.")

The masses don't read editorials, but policy wonks, community leaders, and other governmental types devour them. Sometimes they're quoted in ads (for example, the *Idaho Statesman* says . . .). Depending on your goals, it can be worthwhile to convince a newspaper that your opinion should be its position. You do this by lobbying editorial page staff.

Each newspaper has its own process for making decisions about the content of editorials. At many newspapers, the publisher—in consultation with an "editorial board"—is technically in charge of deciding which editorials are printed and what positions the newspaper advocates in them. This board may consist of the paper's editor, editorial page editor, and others.

In practice, the editorial page editor and editorial writers usually make most decisions relating to editorials unless a high-profile issue such as the endorsement of a major political candidate is involved. At larger newspapers, editorial writers are assigned issue areas (such as education or the environment) and are responsible for writing the paper's editorials on those issues.

At many newspapers, such as the *Cleveland Plain Dealer* and *Seattle Times*, the editorial writers and editors meet each morning to discuss editorials. These journalists present ideas for editorials and analyze both sides, often playing devil's advocate with one another. They strive for consensus.

"The writer makes the case to the rest of the staff about what the position of the paper should be," says Jim Vesely, associate editorial page editor of the *Seattle Times*. "Often, but not always, the writer's position prevails."

Most editorials are written one to three days in advance of publication, but sometimes they can be written a week or more in advance. Editorial writers are usually working on a weekend piece on Wednesday or Thursday. On Friday, they're writing a Monday piece.

As you interact with editorial page staff, keep their deadlines in mind and be aware of how busy they are. "Just as we understand that groups want to be heard, they have to understand that we are inundated with requests to meet with us," says Brent Larkin, editorial page director of the *Cleveland Plain Dealer*.

Tips for Initiating Contact with Editorial Page Staff

- First, familiarize yourself with the position the newspaper has taken on your issue in the past.
- Then, find the e-mail address of the editorial writer who specializes in your issue. To get his or her name and e-mail address, dial the main number of a newspaper and ask for the editorial page.
- Large metropolitan dailies may have five editorial writers plus the editorial page editor. A smaller paper may have only one.
- Once you've identified the right person, briefly explain your position in a short e-mail and ask if he or she would like to (1) receive information by mail or e-mail, (2) talk on the phone, or (3) arrange an in-person meeting.
- If you do not receive a response to your e-mail within a couple of days, call. "Don't be hesitant to pick up the phone and give us a call," says Vincent Carroll, editorial page edi-

tor of the *Rocky Mountain News*, adding that "persistence pays."

Tips for Briefing Editorial Page Staff

Most likely, your briefing will consist of a conversation—either by phone or at the newspaper's office—with the editorial writer who's assigned to your issue. If you have an in-person meeting, you'll likely sit down with an editorial writer—and possibly the editorial page editor and the beat reporter covering your issue. "For a bigger topic, we'll bring in six or seven people plus the publisher," says Jim Vesely at the *Seattle Times*.

- Conduct a practice session before the meeting, responding to difficult questions. (Familiarize yourself with previous editorial positions.)
- For an on-site meeting, take no more than four people. Well-known experts with credentials are great as long as they can explain their views simply. (For a phone briefing, involve only one or two people.)
- Don't expect more than a half hour.
- Bring written materials, even if you've e-mailed them in advance. (See "List of Written Information for Editorial Page Staff" below.)
- If you are working on a national issue and want to simultaneously brief editorial writers at different newspapers around the country, set up a conference call as described in Chapter 18, "News Conferences and Media Kits."
- Ask what they need from you.
- Don't show videos.
- Offer to submit an op-ed if the editors do not adopt your position. (See the next chapter.)
- Send a follow-up e-mail offering further information.

List of Written Information for Editorial Page Staff

- A one-page summary of your position, including details such as complete titles of laws, phone numbers of experts, numbers of people or acres involved, quantity of materials, and other relevant statistics.

- No more than five pages of credible, concise information, possibly including a report summary, an opinion article, photos, and fact sheets. (Follow up with a phone call the subsequent week to find out if more material is needed.)

Sample Letter Requesting an Editorial Board Meeting

John Diaz, Editorial Page Editor
San Francisco Chronicle, Via Fax–415–xxx–7708
RE: Editorial Board Visit
Dear Mr. Diaz:

I write to request an editorial board visit on September 21 with two leaders of the Priorities Campaign (www. businessleaders.org). They are:

Ben Cohen, Co-founder of Ben and Jerry's. Ben is president of the Priorities Campaign (www.businessleaders.org), which aims to increase federal funding for education, health care, and other local priorities. For more information, see our Website at www. businessleaders.org.

Vice Admiral Jack Shanahan (USN, ret.). Jack is the former commander of the U.S. Second Fleet and heads the military advisory committee of the Priorities Campaign.

Ben and Vice Admiral Shanahan would like to discuss federal spending priorities with you. Money is particularly tight in Washington this year, as the budget surplus shrinks and the Bush Administration's tax cut kicks in.

There just isn't enough money to fund everything that our lawmakers from both sides of the aisle want. Something has to give—or Congress will have to borrow money from the Social Security Trust Fund.

The Priorities Campaign believes that Washington's budget squeeze can be solved by trimming the Pentagon budget by 15 percent, freeing up money for the state and local priorities that are on the chopping block. (Even Head Start faces cuts.)

Thanks in advance for considering our request for a meeting.

Jason Salzman
Contact@causecommunications.com
303–292–1524

Responding to an Error in an Editorial

Editorial writers are usually around longer than politicians; consequently, you should avoid destroying long-term relationships over errors or differences of opinion. If an error is made, call the editorial writer, set the facts straight, and send sources of accurate information. He or she may advise you to submit a letter to the editor, which may make sense depending on the gravity of the mistake.

"Everyone will pick up the paper sometimes and feel it's wrong," says editorial writer Steve Millard at the *Boulder Daily Camera*. "But keep criticism from reaching the point of hostility."

Over the long term, keep editorial writers informed, but don't bury them with information. It's probably not worth sending ongoing publications such as newsletters to editorial page writers unless they request them. If you do send such information to local newspapers, it should probably address regional or local issues. Writers say they may "scan" or "glance at" newsletters. Digital versions of all information works best.

Tips for Briefing Reporters

"News briefings" allow you to educate journalists of all types (reporters, producers, columnists, and so on) about your issue—not necessarily because you expect to make the next day's newspaper but simply to inform them. Briefings are best organized when your issue is relevant (that is, it's in the news or will be). They are fixtures in Washington, D.C., where all types of interest groups beg journalists to attend presentations either by conference call or in person. But these briefings occur at the local level as well.

- Stage a briefing around a talk by an expert or group of up to four experts.
- Leave time for questions and conclude the event after forty-five minutes.
- Practice the presentations and answers to tough questions in advance.

- Pitch the briefing as you would a media event (See Part 3, "How to Stage a Media Event"), focusing on journalists who would cover your issue. Take reservations with the understanding that a "yes" can be a tentative commitment.
- Tell reporters you will have light food (continental breakfast) and beverages, but this is not essential.
- Display first-rate visuals.
- Consider holding a briefing by conference call, allowing busy journalists to "attend" from their desks in different parts of the country—and allowing you to involve experts from anywhere. (See Chapter 14, "News Conferences.")
- Prepare handouts like those for an editorial board meeting. If possible, e-mail these materials to attendees in advance. (See "Sample Letter Requesting an Editorial Board Meeting" above.)

23

Write a Guest
Opinion (Op-Ed)

Publishing a guest opinion in the newspaper helps legitimize both your cause and you as a knowledgeable spokesperson for it. Also, a published opinion may turn out to be an excellent position paper for distribution to policymakers, the public, and funders.

These opinion pieces are commonly called op-eds because they're typically published opposite the editorial page. The op-ed page may also contain columns by the paper's regular columnists and by nationally known writers. The latter are distributed electronically to papers across the country; thus your op-ed could run alongside Pat Buchanan's. Imagine that.

Some papers accept opinion columns for publication in other sections of the newspaper, such as the business section. Keep an eye open for these opportunities. Also look for audio commentaries (like those on *All Things Considered*).

For local newspapers, op-eds are most likely to be published if they offer a fresh perspective on a local or regional issue. If you write about national or international issues, try to connect them somehow to local concerns.

If you want to place a piece in a national news outlet, you'll have the most success focusing on a national issue or trends in many communities. Especially at national outlets, the faster you can submit your op-ed in response to the issue you are addressing, the more likely your op-ed will be accepted. Op-eds are frequently published in national papers with opinions about news that was announced the day before—or even in response to news that's in the same issue of the paper.

Tips for Writing Op-Eds

- Aim for 650–700 words.
- Write in the active voice with short paragraphs.
- A piece signed by a well-known expert or personality is more likely to be published. This means that you should consider recruiting someone to sign your op-ed and assist him or her in writing it.
- Try not to be ponderous. Easy-to-read pieces are preferred.
- It's more likely your op-ed will be accepted if your view is different from the newspaper's editorial position. "On op-eds, we give preference to people who disagree with us," says Jim Vesely, associate editorial page editor at the *Seattle Times*.
- Op-eds should address current issues in the news— though sometimes a less current, more philosophical essay will be accepted.
- Be controversial, ironic, and funny, if you can.
- Op-eds rarely break news. They respond to news that's already been reported. Neither do they announce events, products, or initiatives.
- Write a headline with the name of the author under it. Identify the author in a fifteen-word tag line at the bottom.
- Type the number of words in the upper right-hand corner.

Tips for Submitting Op-Eds

Here are two strategies for submitting an op-ed. You can simply write the piece and submit it. This is usually the best option. However, you can also try "querying" editors first, which means that you drop them a one-paragraph e-mail outlining your idea. They will probably e-mail you back saying that they are willing to take a look at it. This brief exchange makes it more likely that they will pay attention to your submission later when you e-mail it to them.

- Submit your piece via e-mail to the op-ed editor. This is the person who decides, sometimes with other editors' input, which opinion columns appear in the paper. At larger papers, you might try the deputy op-ed page editor—who may be more responsive. (For a list of editors at top papers, see www.ccmc.org.)
- Write a brief paragraph summarizing your piece (for example, "In the piece pasted below, I argue . . . ") and the credentials of the author (such as title and organizational affiliation with link to a Website).
- Name drop, if possible, when you contact an editor. "I work with Prof. Head, and he suggested I contact you. . . ."
- Make sure your phone number is listed somewhere obvious on your e-mail.
- Paste your op-ed below your introductory paragraph in the body of your e-mail. *Do not attach the op-ed to your e-mail.*
- If the author of the op-ed is very well-known and the subject is timely, you can ask an editor to let you know within twenty-four to forty-eight hours whether he or she will accept the piece. If the author is not-so-well-known, you should give the editor a week and then call to find out the status of the piece. Most editors don't encourage calls, especially at newspapers like the *Boston Globe* and *USA Today*, which receive about 100 unsolicited op-eds per week and publish only a handful. But you should call them anyway, making sure to be polite and aware of deadlines. The best time to call is early in the week and early in the day.
- Editors say that just before the holidays and toward the end of summer are good times to submit op-eds because there is less competition. However, as a rule, you should write a piece when your issue is in the news.
- It's best to e-mail your op-ed to one news outlet at a time. If you choose to send it to more than one outlet simultaneously, indicate in your cover letter that you are doing so.
- Some nonprofit groups buy issue-oriented op-eds and distribute them to newspapers. These include the Progressive Media Project (www.progressive.org) and Writers on the Range (www.hcn.org). Consider submitting your op-ed to them.

Sample Op-Ed

600 words
Activism Should Be Seen as a Profession
By Jason Salzman

The essential task of political activists—from antiabortionists to disarmers—is to prod citizens to engage in politics. With the world's problems mounting and political apathy growing, activists are needed now, more than ever, to persuade people to become part of the collective solutions to global and local ills. Activists, who may represent causes on the left or right of the political spectrum, are needed to nurture the emergence of our nearly nonexistent political culture.

Political activism and even the word "activist" carry little, if any, legitimacy in our society. To make political activism a more acceptable activity, now is the time to recognize it as a profession.

To do this, it must be made clear that activists are not simply a band of time-warped hippies or the idle rich. Activists are not all desperate, overworked missionaries—so laden with personal problems that they cannot find work in the "for-profit" world. They are not constantly tilting at windmills—though sometimes this is a necessity—or singing folk songs.

Instead, an increasing number of "activists" and workers in the nonprofit sector are qualified professionals who make a livable income doing something they think is important.

Like other professionals, these activists work long but reasonable hours, enjoy their work, and try to apply their skills creatively.

If activism is to be considered a profession, even a lowly one, it also must be recognized that the work of an activist involves skills that take time to develop, though they are often learned on the job rather than in ivory towers.

An activist develops sophisticated public relations skills, including an ad designer's sense of slogans and imagery and an ability to communicate with all elements of society. By the nature of their work, activists develop the skills of fund-raisers, lawyers, researchers, journalists, graphic artists, mediators, scientists, accountants, and teachers. And if nonviolent civil disobedience is required, they are suddenly "criminals" too.

Currently, activism has no ranking as a profession. Activists have no national professional societies, no trade journals, and few professional awards—all of which should be established or augmented. Activism is not even considered on a par with other professions acquired largely through apprenticeship, such as journalism or cooking.

At best, activism is seen as nothing more than a pit stop on the way to a job involving more money, less time, and more real influence.

With undervalued skills and unappreciated importance, activists are sometimes severely underpaid, leading them to burn out and quit. Part of the blame for this must be placed on nonprofit organizations, which in many cases should hire fewer staff at higher pay.

A contributing factor to the social delegitimization of activism is that the traditional tactics of activists (such as rallies, letter-writing campaigns, vigils, even voter-registration drives) are seen as either ineffective or appropriate only for the 1960s.

This has left many citizens with no clue—much less desire—about how to affect politics in our troubled democracy. Ironically, to solve this crisis of democratic expression, we need more activists with professional credibility—regardless of political affiliation—to convince citizens that the traditional and nontraditional tactics of activists, if utilized, are effective and appropriate.

Recognizing activism as a profession would in no way mean that the nonprofessional activist, who is mad as hell about the toxic dump in town, should become a professional activist or shut up. On the contrary, professionals are needed to help sustain the energy of these people—and to help recruit others to become involved.

Jason Salzman is the author of *Making the News: A Guide for Activists and Nonprofits*.

24

Publish (or Broadcast) a Letter to the Editor

Talk back to journalists—and spread the word—by submitting letters to news outlets. The most popular forum for doing this is a newspaper's letters page, which is located in the commentary section near the editorials and op-eds.

But you can also send, fax, or e-mail letters to magazines (*Newsweek*), TV shows (*O'Reilly Factor, Dateline*), radio programs (*All Things Considered*), Websites, and more. Most newspapers and many other news outlets have discussion forums on their Websites where you can post messages about local issues and respond to messages from other readers. And many news outlets also host Web-based "chat rooms," allowing you to interact with journalists and guests.

At the local level the letters pages of area newspapers have the widest appeal to policymakers and citizens. "Letters are very well read," says Marjorie Prichard, op-ed page editor for the *Boston Globe*, adding that groups that focus only on op-eds do themselves a "disservice." "Letters reflect the community. People read the letters page."

It's a lot easier to publish letters to the editor than a longer op-ed. Most local dailies don't run many op-eds by ordinary citizens, and there's keen competition for the limited space available. At the national level, it's even more difficult to publish an op-ed because most guest columns are reserved for well-known writers or officials.

Some newspapers reserve space for letters not only in the editorial or commentary section but also in other sections of the newspaper, such as the business section.

Tips for Writing Letters to the Editor of a Newspaper

- Most papers set a 100–200-word limit for letters.
- Generally, stick to the word limit because it's better that you're in control of what gets cut from your letter than a faceless editor. But also realize that many longer letters appear in print. Try to assess realistically the importance of your letter.
- Write in short paragraphs.
- Put your full name, address, and phone numbers (home and work) at the top of the letter.
- Don't submit form letters.
- Send letters by e-mail, fax, or regular mail. E-mail is best.
- Write in the summer, when there's less competition.
- Read the letters page. You'll know if your brilliant idea occurred to someone else first, and you'll develop an effective letter-writing style.
- Avoid personal attacks.
- Compose your letter with the assumption that readers know nothing about your topic.
- Your letter has the best chance of being published if it's submitted *quickly* and is a reaction to a story in the paper. E-mail your letter, if possible. National outlets, like the *New York Times*, print letters in response to articles that appeared a day or two before.
- Don't assume your idea will be rejected. Most papers don't blacklist ideas.
- Respond directly to other letters to the editor. But you should know that editors usually cut off an ongoing debate on the letters page at some point.
- If appropriate, use software on your Website allowing visitors to send letters directly from your site to news outlets. See, for example, www.saveourenvironment.org.
- Don't write too frequently. There's no rule applicable to all papers, but once every three months is probably about as often as you should write.

- After about ten days, you can call to find out why your letter has not appeared.

Sample Letter to the Editor

Jason Salzman
Rocky Mountain Media Watch
Box 18858
Denver, CO 80218
303-298-1426

May 26, 2003

Letters to the Editor
Newspaper
10 Silver Plume Lane
Motown, CA 94102

Dear Editor:

Congratulations on your decision (5/25/03) to add a weekly column written by a member of our community.

Most everyone appreciates a good sampling of elite punditry. Nationally known columnists generally have lots of experience and connections. But if you're a close pundit watcher, you know that—even though their opinions differ—regular columnists do not add the breadth of diversity that guest writers bring to the opinion pages. Regular pundits observe society from similar, if not identical, places. After all, they're all high-profile pundits.

Guest writers, in contrast, have different jobs and spheres of activity. They don't look at the world and see a column. You could offer more balance on your opinion pages by reserving space for a handful of guest columns each week—and still leave plenty of room for regular pundits.

Sincerely,
Jason Salzman

25

Persuade a Columnist
to Write About Your Issue

Newspapers hire columnists to write opinions—not
the paper's opinion, not your opinion, but the columnists' personal opinions. They do not hire columnists to write fair, balanced articles.

Reporters are supposed to do this. The job of a columnist is to
comment on "issues" in some way, sometimes satirically, sometimes whimsically, sometimes—unfortunately for us—unintelli-
gibly.

Columnists may write monthly, weekly, or four times a week.
Most columnists develop a particular style of writing that becomes familiar to readers over time. They also often write repeatedly about a set of issues or themes, and their opinions on
these issues are frequently predictable.

Learn the Interests and
Styles of Local Columnists

Read as many pieces by local columnists as you can endure, including those that appear in alternative papers. Identify the
columnists who might have an interest in your cause. Then offer them ideas for columns suited to "their issues" and style of
writing.

"I solicit readers' input," says Peter Rowe, a columnist for the
San Diego Union. "I love it. Yesterday, I heard from someone and
I'll be meeting with him and following up on the story tomorrow."

"I'm open to listening to people, as long as they don't have some hare-brained concept that has no base in reality," says Kirk Knox, a columnist for the *Wyoming Tribune-Eagle*.

Tips for Pitching Story Ideas to Columnists

- E-mail a one-page pitch to a columnist and follow-up with a phone call the next day. Have additional information ready to e-mail or fax if the columnist is interested.
- Look for columnists' e-mail addresses at the end of their columns or on the news outlets' Websites. Or call the outlet and ask for it.
- Save your time and theirs by contacting only columnists who might write about an issue like yours.
- On the phone, be brief. Practice your pitch in advance. You should know within a couple of minutes whether the columnist is interested.
- Don't ask for a lunch date. "A lot of times people want to meet with you," says Peter Rowe at the *San Diego Union*. "I don't have a lot of time for meetings."
- Most columnists will not conduct an in-depth investigation on your behalf—primarily because they have too many columns to write and little time and no staff for investigation.
- Columnists will seldom give your group's event—such as a benefit race—free publicity. But be on the lookout for "society" columnists who specifically plug events. You'll see in the paper that they mention community events in their columns.
- Make sure you know if the columnist you want to contact is local or national. Most columns in local newspapers are written by nationally syndicated writers whose work appears in many papers. Look at the end of the column for a tag identifying the columnist. (Think about pitching an idea to a national columnist if you've got a unique story.)
- Consider contacting a columnist who you know disagrees with you about your cause and writes about it frequently. An angry column opposing your position can sometimes kick up a local debate that you will eventually win.

Tips for Keeping Columnists Informed

- If a column contains inaccurate information, e-mail a columnist and present documented, correct information. But remember, it's not a columnist's job to present both sides of a debate. Be reasonable. Remember that columnists are people—not institutions—with whom you should try to develop a respectful relationship. There's a good chance they will be writing columns for many years, outlasting politicians and the day's "hot" issue.

- Columnists don't track breaking news like a reporter—so avoid sending them press releases—but they might be interested to know about a visiting speaker whom they might interview.

- Generally, don't send more than a couple of pages of information to a columnist. Never overwhelm journalists with information.

- Some columnists like to receive newsletters, either by e-mail or snail mail, particularly if they are directly related to issues they write about frequently. Keep in mind that columnists toss most newsletters immediately.

- If a columnist tells a story and pieces of it are left out, let him or her know what's missing. A columnist may come back to your topic later.

- Though a big plus, personal relationships are not essential in convincing a columnist to write about your cause. "I've got to say, my mother keeps giving me story ideas, and I rarely use them," says Peter Rowe at the *San Diego Union*. "And she is a bright, capable person."

26

Influence Newspaper Photographers

Don't leave newspapers' photo departments in the dark-room.

Unlike television journalists, whose medium demands that they constantly think about imagery to accompany their stories, reporters at newspapers don't necessarily make quality photos a priority. Reporters or editors may reject a press release about an event that lacks "news value" without considering carefully whether the event merits a photo.

You can make sure the "photo considerations" of your event are fully weighed by sending press releases—or an idea for a photo—to the photo departments at newspapers. At larger papers, contact the photo assignment editor. Follow up an e-mail or fax with a phone call. "There is no problem with people calling photo departments directly," says Dave Einsel, director of photography for the *Houston Chronicle*. "I don't mind phone calls. I like interacting with the public. It makes life fun."

Reporters and other newspaper staff request photographs to accompany stories they're writing. The photo editor evaluates the requests and assigns the photographers. Sometimes, however, the photo department does not receive enough requests from the news department because communication breaks down—which can happen at any large company—or the shots requested don't make good photographs. The photo department then looks for other photo opportunities. That's why it needs to know about your events and ideas.

- E-mail or fax a news release to the photo editor or individual photographers one to three days prior to your event.
- Place a follow-up phone call when photographers are the least busy: early in the day, Monday through Thursday, or on Sunday morning before the sports events. (Also see Chapter 10, "The Best Times to Get Coverage.") "If we've got nothing else to do, nothing is too stupid," says Dave Einsel at the *Houston Chronicle*. "It's our job to take pictures."
- Don't treat photographers as if they're photo machines or appendages of a reporter. Sometimes they write a piece as well as shoot the event. If you insult their intelligence, it's not as likely that you'll find a photo of your event in the paper, much less a good one.
- Develop a relationship with photographers. Like any other journalists, they can be influenced, and they have the power to suggest shots to their editors. Also, a photo editor or photographer can suggest stories to reporters. "It doesn't hurt to put a photographer who expresses an interest on your mailing list," says Brian Brainerd, a photographer for the *Denver Post*.

27

Sway a Cartoonist

BEING A CARTOONIST IS KIND of a lonely job," says Mike Smith, cartoonist for the *Las Vegas Sun*. "You're kind of a hermit in the far reaches of the newsroom. You're bound up in a room and in your mind. There are so many days I get cabin fever and I'd just like to go outside and walk around. . . . It's nice to know what people are thinking. It's useful to get a perspective of people who are reading the paper, not just the perspective of an editor. It's good to find out what people outside the newsroom are thinking."

Cartoonists at newspapers should hear from you. If a picture is worth a thousand words, a cartoon can be worth millions of them—and a cartoon can be reprinted in a small space and distributed to decisionmakers, supporters, and opponents.

- Cartoonists want information directly related to what's in the news. They deal with what's very current and widely known. You'll notice that most cartoons are simple responses to events. Therefore, it's not useful to send detailed or esoteric information to cartoonists.
- Give information to a cartoonist that highlights an irony or contradiction. This helps cartoonists because, as you can see from reading cartoons, many cartoons highlight paradoxes.
- Tell cartoonists what's going to happen related to your issue. They want tips on upcoming events—hearings, visits by officials. "A reminder of an event [such as national Stop Smoking Week] might be a nudge," says Tom Toles, car-

toonist for the *Buffalo News*. Cartoonist Ed Stein of the *Rocky Mountain News* recalls that numerous employees of the Environmental Protection Agency despised former EPA administrator Ann Gorsuch. Some of these EPA officials would tell Stein when Gorsuch was coming to Denver and give him details of the administrator's policies. He would have a cartoon ready for the paper when she was in town. (Cartoonists, who may draw six cartoons a week at a metropolitan daily, frequently draw pieces the day before publication.)

- "I do want to hear from people if they disagree," says *Denver Post* cartoonist Mike Keefe, acknowledging that this may affect future cartoons. For Keefe, responses are important because he sees discussion about cartoons as advancing, in a "small way," the debate about public policy.

- Don't offer specific ideas for a cartoon. Cartoonists don't want creative help—just information. "People get a thorn in their side and they call," says Smith at the *Las Vegas Sun*. "Everyone's got the Pulitzer Prize–winning cartoon. . . . I don't think I've ever used an idea from someone who's called."

- Complain to a cartoonist about cartoons based on inaccurate information. At that point, give the cartoonist the facts by e-mail—and call later if you do not get a response by e-mail.

- On occasion, let a reporter or an editorial writer know that a piece was "fair and accurate." But don't try this on a cartoonist. Cartoonists want to have the facts straight, but unlike for reporters, professional standards don't demand that they be fair.

- Read a cartoonist's work in the paper and send information that's related to the topics that seem to interest her most. Cartoonist Toles at the *Buffalo News* says: "Personally, I tend to pay attention to environmental suggestions because it's of interest to me and it's an area that's underreported."

28

Tune Your
Cause to Talk Radio

TALK RADIO CAN BE A political and social force. It attracts a
devoted band of listeners, particularly older people who are active in their communities and vote. If you've got the right subject
and an articulate spokesperson, you should use talk radio shows
to get your message out.

Before contacting radio stations, save your own time and the
time of the talk-show staff by learning which programs might air
an issue like yours. Listen to as much talk radio as you can without going crazy. Different shows focus on different themes—
sports, health, current affairs, astrology, cars, and much more.

"Do some research," advises David Lauer, producer of the
Mike Rosen Show for Denver's KOA-AM radio. "I get many offers
for guests that just don't have a chance."

Tips for Booking a Guest on Talk Radio

- Once you've identified an appropriate show for your issue,
  call the radio station and ask for the name and e-mail address of the *producer* of that show.
- E-mail a one-page description of your topic and guest. State
  the dates you've got available.
- Call the producer the next day after sending your
  e-mail. Ask if he or she received your e-mail, and pitch
  your guest.

- Give as much advance notice as you can—up to a month—although typically shows book guests a week in advance, and sometimes the day before a show. So it's never too late to try for most shows.
- If you know a host personally, contact him or her directly. The producer may book the guest right away or discuss the booking with the host and get back to you. "We think about whether it will reach our target audience," says Leonard Nelson at KNBR radio.
- If the producer is not interested, take no for an answer. "Losing gracefully is appreciated," says Lauer at KOA radio. "I'll be more receptive next time they call."
- It's rarely worth sending your group's informational publications to talk shows. Stick to pitching specific subjects and guests to producers and hosts.
- You've got a better chance at booking a guest in the summer, which tends to be a slower time of year. The week after Christmas can also be slow.

Tips for Talk-Radio Interviews

- Any show—even if it has a hostile host—can be a good opportunity to publicize your issue. But don't book a mediocre spokesperson on any show.
- Become familiar with the host and the format of the show in advance.
- Your voice will sound much better if you're interviewed from the studio rather than from a phone. You'll be kept on the air longer, too.
- Tell your supporters to call or e-mail the show when you're on the air, especially if you expect to face a belligerent host, and to monitor various shows and call when your issue is being discussed.
- Ask a friend to tape the show so that you can critique your performance later.
- Arrive at the station a few minutes early.
- Bring some notes with you, but don't read a statement.

- If you have a dynamite audio piece available, bring it to the station and ask that it be played on the air.
- Warm up your body and your voice before you go on the air. Babble for a few minutes or sing. Loosen your facial muscles. Stretch as if you were going jogging.
- Ask for headphones.
- Once you're in the studio, get to know the host. Chat during commercial breaks and before going on the air. But refrain from talking about your subject with the host in the studio. You may forget once you're on the air what you've already covered in the studio.
- Announce your organization's name and Website on the air.
- Don't answer questions with a simple yes or no. Explain your position and have an exchange with the host.
- Summarize numbers. For example, say "just over a third" instead of "33.9 percent."
- Use vocal inflections and avoid "ah" and "ahm." Clarity, emotion, and intensity make good talk radio. (Check out the movie *Talk Radio* for a depressing, if overly dramatic, look into the emotional world of talk radio.)
- Talk at a natural speed. Especially avoid speaking toooo slooooowly.
- Get angry only if you've made a rational decision that it's the right tactic. If your host is quarrelsome, try humor as an antidote. Don't be defensive.
- Ask the host questions. This makes the interview more conversational and takes away the momentum from a host who is attacking you.
- Don't be hesitant to speak over a caller. Many stations have technology that allows your voice to come through over a caller's.
- Try to achieve an intimacy on talk radio, as if you're talking one-on-one to a friend.

29

Place Your TV Production or Information on Cable

THE COMMUNITY ACCESS CENTER IN Kalamazoo, Michigan, broadcasts a program—called *Doggy in the Window*—produced by a local animal shelter. Dogs available for adoption are presented on the show. The Community Access Center doesn't charge the animal shelter anything to air the program on a cable access channel or to use the equipment necessary to produce it.

Since *Doggy in the Window* hit the cable wire, the shelter's adoption rate for dogs has doubled, saving thousands of animals.

Community Access Television of Salina, Kansas, places a notice—submitted by a local food bank—on its televised community bulletin board that a specific food item is needed. The food bank has to run a second notice, stating that it has all of that particular kind of food that it can handle.

If cable television is available in your area, it's likely that at least one cable channel—called the public access channel—broadcasts information from citizens and nonprofit organizations.

Most staff at public access channels around the country are eager to help citizens and nonprofits. "We're in the business of facilitating the public and nonprofit use of the [cable access] channels by training people to create television productions," says Roxanne Earnest, administrative coordinator for Community Access

Television of Salina, Kansas. "In essence, it's communication of, by, and for the public."

What Is Cable Access?

Cable television consists of multiple TV channels that are wired into people's homes on a cable. Once installed, cable television increases the number of channels on a television set by hundreds. Citizens also receive these channels via satellite.

Cable operators such as AT&T or Cablevision offer TV viewers cable "packages." Different cable packages include different mixes of well-known cable channels such as Arts and Entertainment (A&E), Cable News Network (CNN), Cable National Broadcasting Company (CNBC), Nickelodeon, Discovery, the Learning Channel, the Shopping Network, Music Television (MTV), movie channels, weather channels, sports channels, and foreign language channels. Cable packages also offer viewers the capability to pay for movies and events on a pay-as-you-view-them basis.

Installing the network of wires for cable television in a city is a major public works project, much like installing telephone lines, making it essentially impossible for more than one cable operator to offer its services to viewers. As a result, city governments around the United States contract with one cable operator to offer services to residents.

To select a cable company, most city governments solicit competitive proposals and, eventually, negotiate a contract with the company offering the best proposal to provide citywide cable services for a fixed number of years. A cable company's contract with a city typically specifies that one or more channels will be dedicated to the dissemination of public information. These channels are called "access" channels. Cable contracts usually stipulate that cable operators will provide funds (often based on a percentage of income from cable services) for the management of these access channels and the production of programming for them.

The number of public access channels varies from city to city, ranging from none to eight or more. A large city typically has three: a *government access* channel for broadcasting city government hearings or other municipal programs; *an education access* channel for programs, including courses, produced by schools or colleges; and a *public access* channel for broadcasting noncommercial programs produced by citizens and nonprofit organizations.

Some companies, like the DISH Network, offer the typical cable channels via satellite to consumers across the country who install a small satellite receiver on their homes. These satellite networks have public access stations (like Free Speech TV on DISH) that reach a national audience.

Submit Calendar Listings

Most access stations—public or government—produce a "Community Bulletin Board" listing nonprofit services and events. The bulletin board is sometimes broadcast for many hours during the day or at night. Commercial notices are not accepted.

Many access channels have forms available for submissions to their bulletin boards. Call to obtain the proper forms.

Broadcast Independently Produced Programs

Most public access stations will broadcast—for free—programs produced by nonprofits or citizen activists. Any member of the community can submit professionally produced pieces.

Staff at the access channels say they prefer videos that have a local focus, but programs with a national perspective are often accepted as well. Shorter programs about national subjects (up to ten minutes) are more readily accepted than longer ones (up to an hour or more). And any national piece is more likely to be aired if submitted by a local group.

Most public access channels do not allow commercial advertising or monetary solicitations. For example, a church may be able to air a program with religious content, but it could not ask for donations. This rule, like other generalizations about access channels, may vary from city to city.

Produce Your Own Program

You can also learn how to operate camera equipment, edit film, and produce your own show for your local public access station.

Most offer classes, equipment, and a time slot for your program, depending on availability. This training probably won't run more than $50 and could cost you nothing. Unfortunately, producing video is time-consuming, especially for busy nonprofit staff. A regular program, in particular, can chew up large chunks of time. One way to clear this obstacle is to have volunteers—or student interns—do the show. Another option: Some cable companies will produce a one-time program for nonprofits at minimal cost.

Who Watches Cable Access?

The major downside of using cable access is that relatively few people tune to it—even though about a third of U.S. citizens subscribe to cable television. One reason: The access channels are usually in the fifties on the TV dial (for example, channel 54), well away from the zone of most channel surfers. Also, the quality of programming—precisely because much of it is produced by citizens and nonprofit organizations—is usually spotty. In addition, most of the access programming isn't publicized or even listed in TV schedules. Many access channels have no programming (literally, they have a static-filled screen) for much of the day.

If your target audience is watching cable access, you should consider using it. Community access staff say citizens interested in local government watch. Others say seniors follow it. Try to find out from staff at your local access channel who tunes in your area. You might have to take a plunge and see what happens. The animal shelter in Michigan that doubled its adoption rate for dogs after it began its *Doggy in the Window* program probably had no idea the show would be successful before trying.

30

Use Community
Calendars and Public
Service Announcements

Find out which news organizations in your media market have calendars listing community events and become familiar with them. You'll discover that newspapers have the widest selection, often featuring distinct listings for entertainment, business, sports, religion, and more. Alternative weeklies would not be alternative weeklies without calendar listings. And many cities have Web-based sites listing local entertainment and other events.

Calendar editors want to hear from you. Getting your information is their job.

E-mail a truncated press release to calendar editors, clearly stating the essential information about your event: who, what, where, when, and a contact name and phone number. (See Chapter 14, "News Releases.")

"Just yesterday, I was looking at a wonderful poster about an event, but it didn't have any location or time on it," says Kim Tondryk, editorial assistant at the *Milwaukee Journal Sentinel*. "That's the information I need."

Also send art or photos that can be used to illustrate your event. Community groups don't send in enough quality photos or illustrations to calendar editors. Find out if your photo requires a signed release form. Sometimes calendar editors have to "scrounge" for art or photos. You never know if your photo—even if you think it's weak—will be needed.

Tips for Getting Listed in Community Calendars

- Get your information in on time. You should send most releases at least two weeks in advance, but earlier is better. Different calendars in the same paper have different deadlines—one for a music magazine, another for a Sunday events calendar, and yet another for the religion section.
- Ask if color photos are accepted and in what format they should be submitted.
- Call calendar editors to find out about deadlines and special needs.
- Double check your information. Calendar editors are brimming with stories about wrong dates, phone numbers, and so on.
- Generally, e-mail your information. But you should find out how specific outlets want to receive it. Some prefer a fax.
- Don't phone in your item. "We don't take anything over the phone because of the volume I get on a weekly basis," says Kim Tondryk at the *Milwaukee Journal Sentinel*. (She gets 400 to 600 pieces of mail per week.)
- Some editors advise *not* calling to make sure they received your information, but you should call anyway. Over time you will know whom you don't need to bother with a follow-up call.
- Don't forget that your local cable-access TV station probably has a listing of upcoming events. (See previous chapter.)
- At radio stations, call the DJs directly and ask them to read your announcement on the air. Call DJs at any radio station on each shift—even if they don't normally read the news. This works. I've persuaded dozens of DJs to plug rallies and events.

Public Service Announcements (PSAs)

Public Service Announcements, primarily aired by TV and radio news outlets, either describe a nonprofit event or a nonprofit program, like a blood drive or tutoring program. They run 15 to 30 seconds, and most often you see or hear them at odd hours, like the middle of the night. Even so, they reach a large audience.

Trouble is, not many of them are used and, if so, they're about milk-toast issues, which means you can forget about submitting anything political—unless you focus on community radio stations or other outlets that cater to a market segment that matches your political beliefs.

"We really like to show PSAs that are anti-drug or deal with fatherhood, mentoring, issues like that," said Elaine Harrison, public service director for WVLA-TV in Baton Rouge, Louisiana.

If you want give this a try, the best advice is to call the public service or community relations director at your local TV station. Or e-mail the news director at a radio station. Ask what kinds of PSAs are accepted (length, format) and if your idea sounds promising. Involving a local or national celebrity can be helpful.

You will need professional help to create a broadcast-quality PSA. You might find an advertising firm or a volunteer to do this for free. Some national nonprofits hire consultants to produce PSAs and distribute them nationally. But news outlets generally prefer spots focusing on local issues.

"Typically, we run PSAs that we produce in conjunction with an organization," says Bronwyn Pope, director of public relations at WCCO-TV in Minneapolis. "If we have more time to fill, we might use one that is sent in. But the best way is to work with us."

If you have an entertaining PSA dealing with a hot issue, hold a news conference if it's rejected because it's "too controversial" or "not in the public interest." This could turn your PSA into news. You could reach far more people this way than you ever would if your PSA had been accepted. (See Part One, "Stop Being a Bore.")

31

Publicize a Report
or Academic Paper

THIS CHAPTER IS FOR ACADEMICS who write papers and reports *and* nonprofit groups or activists who do the same. Open any newspaper and you'll see how the news media feed on quantifiable information and new research data (for example, "An article in *Science* magazine, published today, reveals that . . . ").

Statistics on almost any topic of interest can be big newsmakers: crime rates, consumer patterns, sales, polls, and so forth. Soon-to-be-published findings from journals are a major news source. Nonprofit organizations take advantage of information-hungry reporters by releasing reports and polls of their own. For example, the Center for Science in the Public Interest draws lots of media attention for its studies of the fat content of Chinese food, diet foods, and other comestibles. Data about almost any concern—from the environment to homelessness—can be news.

To the chagrin of serious scientists, journalists sometimes cover pseudoscientific reports—based on humorous or quirky anecdotal information—with the same gusto as they do reports based on years of careful research. The simple report could easily have gotten more attention than a ten-year study of illiteracy: A Yale professor wrote a report, sponsored by Procter & Gamble and released in conjunction with a new shampoo, concluding that bad hair days make people sad.

In any case, the fact remains that reports with quantifiable information and a scientific seal of approval are attractive to journalists. The key is to simplify and explain the information so that it meets their needs. Also, like most people in our TV culture, broadcast journalists want images to accompany data. Your report with powerful statistics may be covered in every newspaper in the country, but without an image that can carry it to the tube, the effect on many people will be muted. Numbers crack the back door to the news, but images blow the door open.

News-Induced Headaches and Tips on How to Avoid Them

Many careful researchers and writers are frustrated by the news and choose to avoid journalists altogether. Journalism can fall short of the exacting standards set by detail-oriented people for the following reasons:

- News seldom offers more than two opposing opinions, even though most issues have many sides to consider. Unfortunately, journalists lack space for more information, and many don't seek other views because their job is widely considered done when two sides are captured.
- Journalists value simple information, whereas reality is complex. As a result, some stories are completely shut out of the news, especially television news, and others are simplified to the point of being meaningless.
- Journalists downplay uncertainty, especially in headlines. Just the presence of an article in a newspaper—regardless of what it says—implies certainty.
- Between deadline pressures and staff cuts, the facts inevitably get twisted sometimes despite the best efforts of journalists.
- Science is overshadowed by personalities and politics. The substance of many debates in the news takes a backseat to who's winning and what that person is doing.
- Crisis coverage is emphasized. This means that many important issues are ignored until a crisis occurs. How much coverage do you see of African poverty until starvation strikes or a war starts?
- News is image-based and event-centered. Issues and ideas that don't lend themselves to visual imagery are often shut out of the news.

- Quotations can be distorted. Sound bites are sometimes incapable of expressing truth.

You cannot avoid all of these headaches because many arise out of the nature of journalism. But here are some ways to relieve, if not eliminate, many of them.

- Don't leave it to journalists to simplify your complex information. Recognize journalistic realities and simplify your information for them.
- Know deadlines and give journalists enough time to review your information. Don't force journalists to make mistakes because they are rushing. (See Chapter 10, "The Best Times to Get Coverage.")
- Tell a journalist the name of someone who "opposes" your position. If you supply a reasonable "other side," you lessen the likelihood that a reporter will quote a quack who opposes you.
- Don't overwhelm journalists with information, especially written information. Think about the limited space journalists work with and decide precisely what slice of your information you want them to use. (See the next section.)
- Tell journalists directly, perhaps at the end of an interview, what you think is the most important aspect of your report.
- Accept the event-centered nature of news and turn the release of your report into an event, using an appropriate visual. For example, if your report is about frogs, make some frogs available for photographers at a news conference. Highlight the planned appearance of the frogs in your news release.
- Take advantage of "crisis coverage" by releasing your information when the media is focusing on a crisis related to your expertise. If there's an oil spill and you've got data showing that routine oil leaks are a more serious threat than large spills, release your data when coverage is focusing on the crisis.
- Don't take journalism too seriously. A mistake or a distortion in the news media isn't that big a deal (though in some cases internal politics at a university or elsewhere demand caution). Just keep trying to get the word out. It's the cumulative efforts that count.

If you are willing to accept some of the hazards and limitations of journalism and want to publicize your report in the news media, use Part Three of this book as your guide for releasing your report to the news media. The nuts and bolts for attracting media attention to a report are identical to those for drawing the media to an event. Your goal should be to turn the release of your report into a *media event*.

Tips for Making a Report More Newsworthy

- Develop a short (three to ten pages), executive summary. Make the full report available upon request.
- Upload your executive summary and full report to a Website and list the site's address on your news release.
- In a news release, emphasize just a few statistics. Remember, most news stories don't cover many points.
- Use clear, attractive graphs or tables and short paragraphs without jargon.
- Connect your report to a news hook. (See Chapter 21, "Hook Your Story to Breaking News.")
- If possible, show a change in data from the previous year.
- Create quirky titles for trends or other data (for example, "gender gap").
- Rank the objects of your study, if possible, and give awards.
- If you are affiliated with an academic institution, take advantage of the public relations office at most universities for media contacts and other help. Print your news release on university letterhead.
- Make numbers more meaningful by using comparisons or breaking them down into units that are more comprehensible. (For example, Business Leaders for Sensible Priorities points out that America spends $395 billion on the Pentagon, over $1 billion per day. So, just ten days of Pentagon spending is equal to the total amount of America's humanitarian foreign aid budget.)
- Localize news releases about a national report and send them directly to local journalists. (An Environmental Defense Fund report showed that most U.S. endangered

UNITED≥FAIR ECONOMY.

Press Advisory - April 4, 2002
Contact: Betsy Leondar-Wright
(617) 423-2148 x13

New report: Harmful Enron practices widespread

Awards to most Enron-like companies

On April 10, United for a Fair Economy will release a report by **Error! Bookmark not defined.** called *Titans of the Enron Economy: The 10 Habits of Highly Defective Corporations.*

Most of Enron's harmful behavior was perfectly legal. UFE has identified ten elements of the Enron story practiced by other major American corporations:

Risks for workers, rewards for executives
1. Retirement funds full of company stock
2. Excessive CEO pay
3. Massive layoffs while executives make millions

Corrupting the watchdogs
4. Insider boards
5. High board compensation
6. Auditors with consulting contracts that create conflicts of interest

Profiting from political influence
7. Hefty political contributions to buy access
8. Lobbying for legislative favoritism
9. Corporate welfare to finance dubious overseas investments
10. Avoidance of corporate taxes

The report will **rank the worst companies on each Enron-like habit.** UFE will bestow an **Enny Award** to a company with especially egregious behavior in each area.

An overall **Lifetime Achievement Enny** will go to the corporation with the highest combined score for Enron-like performance in all 10 categories. Sneak preview: it's not Enron!

The report will be available on the web at www.FairEconomy.org on April 10.

THE ENNY

###

37 Temple Place, 2nd floor, Boston, MA 02111
(617) 423-2148, fax (617) 423-0191
website www.FairEconomy.org, e-mail bleondar-wright@FairEconomy.org

A potentially boring report on corporate evils is presented to media in entertaining and simple language. CREDIT: UNITED FOR A FAIR ECONOMY

species could be saved if key areas in the United States were protected. It crafted news releases for media outlets near those key areas.)

- In addition to releasing your report to the news media, consider publishing a short summary of it as a guest opinion in the newspaper. (See Chapter 23, "Write a Guest Opinion (Op-Ed).")

32

Promote a Story to Journalists at National News Outlets

JOURNALISTS AT NATIONAL NEWS outlets are busier and harder to reach than their local counterparts. Otherwise, the keys to promoting a story at the national level are largely the same as promoting a story at the local level.

This holds true whether you're trying to access news reporters, talk-radio producers, TV talk-show producers, TV "news magazine" producers, newspaper columnists, feature writers, editorial page editors, or any journalist at a national outlet. (You can also persuade photo editors at national news magazines to buy photos of events. This is easier if you hire a professional "freelance" photographer to shoot photos for you. Photos taken by your organization aren't as easily sold to photo editors.)

Most of the same techniques apply: Keep it simple, know deadlines, be professional, contact the right person at appropriate media outlets, have the proper written information, use contacts, and study the tips in this book.

"Particularly for *Newsweek*, the threshold is higher," says Michael Hirsh, an international correspondent for *Newsweek*. "It's got to illustrate a trend as opposed to a tidbit."

If you live in a major metropolitan area, a national news outlet might have a bureau with staff in your city. If so, try to pitch your story to journalists there. For example, the *NewsHour with Jim Lehrer* has a bureau in Denver. NBC News has one in Chicago. To find out whether there are bureaus or stringers (local representatives who file occasional stories) in your area, call the outlet's headquarters and check the yellow pages of the phone book or directories (online or in the library) listing national news media. For stringers, also ask people familiar with your local media market.

If a national news outlet doesn't have a bureau or stringers in your city, call its regional bureau, if possible. Then try an outlet's headquarters.

If you are focusing on a national outlet's main office and you don't have a contact, you should obtain a comprehensive list of staff at your target program (such as *Good Morning America* or *O'Reilly Factor*) or target newspaper section (*New York Times* Business Section or *Washington Post* Style Section), and start making calls. At national TV outlets or newspapers, first try *assistant* producers or *assistant* editors, who are often easier to reach than senior editors or producers. Try to get *any staffer* to give you a name of a colleague who might be interested in your story. Call him or her, and say something like, "Jackie Blum said you might be interested in . . ."

You'll be amazed at how the national media follow each other. Once your story is covered by one outlet, others will come. "I can pitch a story here [to other journalists at CNN] until I'm blue in the face—until it appears in the *New York Times*," says Peter Dykstra, a senior producer at CNN. "Then the response is, 'Why haven't you been on top of this?'"

Tomi Ervamaa, a Washington, D.C.–based correspondent for *Helsingin Sanomat*, a major paper in Finland, says, "We steal ideas from each other. I read the *New York Times* and *Washington Post* to get ideas."

Associated Press Is a Gateway to National Coverage

News outlets from around the country "subscribe" to news services, which—in return—transmit news stories, photos, video, and other information to their subscribers. The subscribers can use information from news services in their broadcasts or publications. The quantity and type of information that news outlets receive from news services vary according to the type of subscription they buy. For example, a news service might have a menu of news available, including sports, weather, business, and statewide, national, and international news.

The largest news service in the United States is the Associated Press (AP), which is the heart of America's newsgathering system. The most likely way that your story will be distributed beyond your city—either regionally or nationally—is via the AP.

The AP is a not-for-profit corporation owned by the 1,500 newspaper members that subscribe to it. Over 5,000 other news outlets, like radio and TV stations, subscribe as well. AP's members and AP exchange news stories with each other, meaning that AP's members may use AP's news stories and AP may distribute its members' news to other members and subscribers around the world.

AP does not cover many local stories with its own reporters, taking them instead from newspapers. "The San Francisco bureau does not cover the city of San Francisco," says Bill Schiffmann, broadcast editor for AP's San Francisco bureau. "We let local papers cover it. If it's something of state-wide interest, we'll take it out of the paper the next morning. We only cover stories that are of interest nationally."

Even when AP does assign a reporter to cover a local story, local newspapers tend *not* to use AP coverage, preferring stories written by their own staffs.

But newspapers large and small often rely heavily on AP for news about national or international topics. Thus your story on the AP wire may be used in every newspaper across the country *except* your local one. In contrast, local broadcast media, especially radio stations without news reporters on staff, rely on AP stories for both local and national news. Many radio DJs read AP news exclusively.

The AP in the United States is divided into "bureaus." (There are 146 bureaus in America and ninety-five internationally.) Typically an AP bureau has a bureau chief, who's in charge. Under him are an assistant bureau chief and a news editor, who assigns stories to reporters. Larger bureaus may have business, sports, photo, and other editors who cover specific issue areas. A correspondent, who reports to the bureau chief, is in charge of smaller

AP offices and may have reporters working under him or her. The New York and Washington, D.C., offices of AP employ reporters and editors covering every type of national and international news you can think of.

A bureau may be responsible for covering news in one or more states or a large metropolitan area. For example, the San Francisco bureau has twelve staff. Colorado and Wyoming are lumped in one bureau with "correspondents" in Cheyenne (four), Grand Junction (one), and Denver (ten). Colorado news media that subscribe to AP generally receive at least the stories about Colorado and Wyoming from the Colorado-Wyoming bureau, which may transmit fifty to sixty pieces per day via computer, plus about six photos. Some news outlets, such as regional newspapers, subscribe to other states' AP wires.

If the Colorado-Wyoming, San Francisco, or any other AP bureau believes that one of its stories is of national interest, it forwards the story to the national news "desk" in New York. Editors there decide whether it's placed on the national wire—to be sent to AP subscribers around the country.

If a story from a bureau is of international interest, it is sent to the foreign desk in New York or Washington, D.C. From there, it could be zapped around the world. There are multiple foreign wires covering different regions of the world. Stories on some of these wires are translated into different languages. (Read more about the Associated Press and other news services in Chapter 15, "Distributing a News Release.")

Six Ways to Increase Your Chances of AP Coverage

1. AP is a service that responds to its members and subscribers, which are thousands of news media outlets that pay a fee to receive AP stories, photos, video, and more. If you can persuade an AP subscriber to request a photo or story from an AP office, your chances of getting covered are greatly increased. To do this, you need to persuade a reporter, who will not attend your event, to request that AP cover it. A reporter in another city or state could do this. For example, once a Greenpeace colleague persuaded a reporter in South Carolina to request an AP photo of a Den-

ver protest that was relevant to a current issue in South Carolina. Sure enough, an AP photographer attended our protest and a photo was distributed nationally.

2. AP often runs stories on its national wire that affect many states. For example, rankings of states or cities according to various comparatives such as "most livable" or "most affluent" are widely distributed by AP. If you are promoting a story with this kind of wide appeal, you should make an extra effort to persuade AP to cover you.

3. Use your contacts. A colleague knew a professor who was a former national editor at AP. We were having problems convincing AP to cover a report, and we called the professor for ideas. He gave us the name of someone in the New York AP office, whom we contacted. The next week our story was distributed nationally by AP.

4. Sometimes AP will buy photos of your event if an AP photographer didn't make it to the event. If you've got a good story, bring your photos to the AP office. A freelance photographer's work is best, but it's not required. (You can also bring your dramatic home video to television stations if they did not show up.)

5. Contact AP photographers directly by fax or e-mail. Then call them. They can make independent decisions on whether an event merits a photograph, which may be distributed to media outlets around the world. "The photo decision is often made separate from the news decision," says David Briscoe at the Associated Press. "Maybe a demonstration is taking place about a routine issue that doesn't merit a news story, but it's visually interesting."

6. Associated Press reporters like to have a news story a little before other news outlets get it so that the story can be distributed before it's officially released. To accommodate AP, you might, for example, give AP your story a day or two before you release it at a news conference on February 17 at 10 A.M. EST. If you have embargoed your story for 8 A.M. EST on the day of your conference, then AP would—you hope—put your story on the wire around 8 A.M. and possibly update it at your 10 A.M. news conference. Prior notice also gives AP the opportunity to schedule a time slot for the

story to be distributed electronically. (See Chapter 14, "News Releases.")

One Example of How a Local
Story Can Become National News

The U.S. Postal Service once announced plans to abandon its historic building in downtown Livingston, Montana, and build a new facility on the edge of town. Local residents objected to the relocation, arguing that a "Wal-Mart style" post office was not appropriate for their town. A group of citizens immediately organized to keep the post office in the existing building, which was listed on the National Register of Historic Places.

The group organized support in town and, with a series of press releases, elevated the issue to the front page of several local papers. The story quickly became statewide news in Montana. Next, the activists identified Montana-based stringers for national publications. They called the journalists and pitched the post office story to them. Not all the national journalists jumped at the story, but bit by bit, interest began to grow, especially after the *New York Times* ran an article about it. *Time* magazine followed, publishing a full-page piece about the campaign titled "It Breaks a Village."

It turned out that citizens in other small U.S. towns were facing the same problem: The post office was abandoning old buildings in favor of large, new facilities. So the Montana story was emblematic of a national trend. This helped convince reporters that the story was worthy of a national audience. Soon pieces about the Livingston post office appeared in the *Washington Post* and the *Christian Science Monitor* and on National Public Radio.

"When the story started appearing in East Coast papers, the postmaster general got upset," says activist Dennis Glick. That's when the tide turned, and the post office announced that it would renovate its downtown Livingston office and build a smaller processing facility out of town. The activists won even though the fight looked impossible at the outset.

Glick says the media campaign was key to their success. "Toward the end, the *Today* show called," he says. "It's funny how this stuff snowballs. Once you get some coverage, it all starts rolling in."

33

Generate News Coverage Abroad

IF YOU'RE PROTESTING THE IMPORTATION of grapes laced with dangerous pesticide residues, your campaign would probably benefit from news coverage in countries that export grapes. To get news coverage abroad, don't rely on U.S. news outlets or services to transmit your story around the world even though some—for example, the Associated Press—have the capability to do this. Contact news media from foreign countries directly.

It turns out that if your story is appropriate, getting international media coverage is not too difficult. In fact, sometimes you'll be able to get more media attention abroad than you'll receive in this country.

Some publicists know this and use it to pressure foreign countries. For example, in the mid–1980s, the New Zealand government banned all U.S. nuclear-powered and nuclear-armed warships from docking in its ports. The Kiwis figured that bringing nuclear bombs to the South Pacific was an example of the Cold War run amok. But the Reagan administration and its allies in Congress didn't see it that way. To punish New Zealand, the administration eventually withdrew the United States from all treaty obligations to come to the aid of its longtime ally down under.

Leading up to the decision to abandon New Zealand, anti–New Zealand forces in Washington stepped up public pressure on the New Zealanders. They knew that the nuclear issue was so sensitive in the United States that any development here would be big news there.

One of the ways they generated huge headlines in New Zealand was to arrange to have introduced a bill in Congress attacking the country, which has about 4 million people and 60 million sheep. The introduction of a bill in the U.S. Congress is a nonevent. It means practically nothing because only a small percentage of bills introduced in Congress are even brought to a vote. (Many are introduced by one crusading member of the House of Representatives who has lined up no co-sponsors for the proposed legislation.) The two-page New Zealand bill introduced in the House called for, among other things, banning all lamb imports from New Zealand! You can imagine the headlines in the Kiwi press. Here, of course, there was only minimal coverage, and there was never a vote on the bill.

A response in the United States—even if it's by a small activist group—to a sensitive issue in a foreign country is usually news there.

"If there's a Dutch angle, I will go for it," says Oscar Garchagen, a reporter for *Devolkskrant*, a major paper in the Netherlands. But he emphasizes that his job is to cover what's happening in the United States, not to focus on issues related to the Netherlands.

"NGOs [non-governmental organizations] are very effective, available, and very helpful," he says. "I use NGOs as a source just as I use government sources."

U.S.-based foreign correspondents are not hard to reach. (See the tips in this chapter.) But like other journalists, they face time constraints and deadline pressures. Often, one reporter has the staggering job of covering the entire United States, including major political events. These reporters should be approached as you would any other busy journalist.

"I do stories about people," says reporter Tomi Ervamaa, a Washington, D.C., reporter for *Helsingin Sanomat*, a large newspaper in Finland. "I try to get out of D.C. and do feature stories about life in the U.S."

Tips for Obtaining Lists of Foreign Journalists

- For a list of news media in a specific country, call the embassy or consulate of that country and ask for it. You can request names of foreign journalists working in the United States as well as in their own country. This does not produce results all the time, but it's worth a try.

- Check international media directories. Bacon's publishes one, but your local library may have others that will work. These directories should list foreign media with U.S. offices. The U.S. State Department also publishes a list of foreign media. (See "Resources.")

- Many large foreign media outlets maintain offices in Washington, D.C., and many are located in the National Press Club on Fourteenth Street, which distributes a list of building occupants.

- Some countries have their own national news services (such as Japan's Jiji Press, Agence France-Presse in France, Yonhap for South Korea, and Xinhau for China), which might be interested in your story and have representatives in the United States. Reuters is Europe's major news service. Focus on these first, as they will distribute your story widely. (For more information on news services, see Chapter 13, "Media Lists.")

- Contact an allied group that promotes stories internationally. As always, it's best not to have to reinvent the media list.

- It's easier to pitch your story to foreign journalists based in the United States—probably in New York, Washington, D.C., or San Francisco—than to journalists abroad. These reporters may not attend your news conference in Austin, Texas, but they might take your story over the phone. They also might be interested in obtaining photos from you. If you're serious and have the proper language skills, you can call abroad or e-mail.

Tips for Attracting Foreign Journalists to a Story

- As described previously, even the most trivial actions by the U.S. Congress can make big news abroad. It's worth the effort to pressure a member of Congress to act—introduce a bill, sponsor a resolution, or even simply write a letter.

- Issue a "reaction" news release containing your quote related to breaking news about a foreign country. Quotes praising foreign countries are often picked up, too. (See Chapter 20, "Suggest Story Ideas to Journalists" and Chapter 21, "Hook Your Story to Breaking News.")
- Have someone from a foreign country "do something" here in the United States (for example, write a report, participate in an event) and feature the foreigner in your press materials—with any other information you want to promote.
- Find out if a U.S. company has foreign partners. If so, you can promote your event related to the U.S. company not only to the U.S. media but also to the media of the country of its partners.
- Bring your own photographers to a meeting with foreign officials and distribute the video or photographs of the meeting to the foreign press with the story.
- Organize a coalition of nonprofit groups or notables (for example, political figures, business leaders, celebrities) to send a joint letter to a foreign government and announce it in a press release. Such letters would receive little or no coverage in the United States but could be news abroad.
- Hold an event (protest, delivery, stunt) at a company, consulate, or embassy of a foreign country. Even a few protesters can make news. For example, Greenpeace organized a rally of about forty people in front of the Taiwan trade mission to protest shipments of nuclear waste from Taiwan to North Korea. The media efforts, which yielded major coverage, focused on China, Taiwan, and Korea. "Even just a few protesters can make news abroad," says Tom Clements of Greenpeace International. "We've had great success getting in the foreign media, even with simple protests in the United States."

Tips for Generating News at an International Summit

Often thousands of journalists from around the world converge on a city to cover a summit or meeting of international leaders. This is an opportunity—although a difficult one—to capture the attention of the world's media.

- Get media credentials. This allows you access to the media headquarters, where you can pitch your story directly to journalists. To get credentials, you may have to apply a month or so in advance. Check for a Website of the international summit you want to attend and look for information on media credentials.
- Find a list of attending journalists. Call the local press office that's set up for the international meeting. Also, stop by the desk where journalists pick up their press credentials and ask for a comprehensive list of journalists who've been granted credentials.
- Identify the hotels where the foreign journalists are staying and deliver news releases there. You can also fax news releases to hotel guests.
- Determine where, in the media headquarters, journalists from various countries have their assigned work stations and deliver news releases to targeted countries.
- Explain in news releases why your story or event would be of particular interest to journalists from specific countries.
- Create a visual image that can be easily accessed by photographers. Often, meetings of international leaders are slim on visuals, so yours could make a hit. Highlight the visual aspect of your event in your news release or flyer, which should be circulated inside media headquarters. Stage your event as close to headquarters as possible.
- Pitch your story directly to journalists whenever possible. Convincing individual journalists of the merits of your story is probably the most effective way to get coverage.
- Use personal contacts. If you know journalists—or if you think specific publications will cover your issue—try them first.
- Hold a local media event or stunt the day before the summit starts. This will put your issue in the local newspaper as foreign journalists arrive in town.

34

Hit the Small-Time: Neighborhood and Rural News

Getting news coverage in smaller media markets requires different tactics than landing big-city attention.

The major difference is that, often, you need to submit fully written stories and photos to editors. The less work they have to do, the better, meaning that you should submit polished copy that reflects their style—not yours. Your story may run exactly as you submitted it.

You need to think local, think local, and then think local again. These outlets want stories that are community-based.

Tips for Making Small-Time News

- Don't assume that rural or smaller communities are served by just one newspaper. A small community may well be served by overlapping local and regional newspapers and radio stations, as well as cable access.
- If you are trying to influence a local journalist to take a position on an issue, find out who can lobby on your behalf. Small communities are close-knit.
- Think twice before going for the theatrical media stunt. Will this appeal to your audience? If not, you can probably get the same amount of coverage with a more conservative approach.

- Write thank-you notes. You need not worry so much that a "thanks" will offend a journalist's professional "objective" sensibility.
- As always, know deadlines, and submit your stories with plenty of time to spare. Make it easy.
- If you are working on a national or state-wide issue, figure out how to localize it. Find a local spokesperson. Document how it will affect local residents. "It has to have a community angle," says M. L. Headrick, staff writer at the *Moody County Enterprise*, Flandreau, South Dakota.
- If appropriate, suggest a regular contribution. For example, after I got to know one editor of a small urban newspaper, I suggested that I write a regular environmental column—which she agreed to.
- Be sure to ask editors whether they like to communicate by e-mail, fax, or snail mail. "Human contact is usually the most effective," says Donald Ward, assistant editor of *The Leavenworth Echo* in Leavenworth, Washington.

Newspapers

Most large cities have at least a handful of suburban or neighborhood newspapers that everyone snickers about but loves to read. Same with small towns. The local rag is devoured as soon as it hits the porch.

Make contact with editors by phone and find out 1) if they want to write about your story themselves or 2) if they want you to submit a story and/or photos. If it's the latter, ask how long they want you piece to be.

"We do accept some submissions [of stories and photos], although those usually don't go on the front pages," says Ward of the *Leavenworth Echo*. "They are usually filler that goes on the inside pages."

If editors want photos, make sure you submit them with accurate captions. Most will prefer digital.

Most of these papers are weeklies, and they are usually published on Wednesdays. It's usually best to submit stories by Friday of the previous week.

Radio

Most small-town radio stations broadcast regular talk-show programs to discuss local happenings and issues. If your issue is timely, local radio will want to cover it. To arrange an interview, call the local host or station manager and make your pitch, emphasizing the local connection and local spokespeople. (Make sure not to overlook nonprofit community radio stations.)

Just as you can write a news story for a small newspaper, you can record a radio piece for small radio stations. These are called "radio actualities," "radio newsfeeds," or "audio news releases (ANR)." They are basically recorded news releases, lasting a minute or so, with a narrator introducing the story and actual soundbites from experts, celebrities, or other newsworthy people. Radio stations can use the entire recording as a news story, or pull out the soundbites and use them separately.

Audio news releases are recorded professionally and transferred to CD or audiocassette. They are then distributed by e-mail, snail mail, or telephone. ANRs can also be made available on Websites or even by satellite.

Most large radio stations will not use ANRs. But smaller stations, especially in rural areas, with limited staff and an interest in covering your issue, will sometimes air parts of them.

Pitch your ANR with a news release and a follow-up call, describing the story and stating that the ANR is available. If the station's news staff is interested, ask how they would like to receive it. If they want it by telephone, you can transmit it using inexpensive equipment.

The most effective ANRs provide simple soundbites relating to breaking news.

Television

Small towns or neighborhoods do *not* have their own trash-and-flash local TV news stations. Many rural citizens watch local TV news via satellite or cable from the nearest large city. And suburbanites watch the TV news from their surrounding metropolis. But television news, which is designed to appeal to a mass audience, does not cover small communities specifically.

Some mid-sized towns, however, do have a cable access station that is watched by residents who subscribe to cable TV. These stations focus on community news and will frequently air documentaries or other taped material that you submit. They list community events and will sometimes have volunteers who will cover community-based events. Some have equipment allowing you to shoot your own community-based events. (See Chapter 29, "Place Your TV Production or Information on Cable.")

When trying to reach any small audience, make sure to consider all your options—beyond making news. Often hand-to-hand marketing, passing out flyers at the supermarket or putting up a table at the local fair, can be as effective or more than trying to get news coverage that reaches your slice of the community.

Part FIVE

Your Cause
in Cyberspace

Techniques for using the Internet to get news coverage are spread throughout this book, for the simple reason that the Internet is integral to PR—from pitching reporters and publishing op-eds to creating spoof Websites. E-mail and Websites are essential tools of the PR trade, whether you work for a two-bit nonprofit or the CEO of Ford.

This section explains how to ensure that your news is heard in cyberspace. It also covers the basics of how to use Websites to communicate effectively with all journalists, not just those who work for an online news outlet.

35

News on the Web

Here's the most important fact that you, as a publicist focusing on the *news media*, should know about news and the Internet: Most news consumed online is produced by reporters who work for traditional "offline" news outlets.

So, the most popular Websites that offer news "content" do not have reporters whom you can pitch. But if you successfully sell your story to journalists at broadcast and print news outlets (for example, TV and radio, newspapers, news services, magazines), as outlined elsewhere in this book, your story will appear on the Web as well.

(There are lots of ways to *market* your cause in cyberspace—using various head-spinning ads, e-mail tricks, listservs, discussion groups, and lots more—but that's the subject of another book. This one focuses on the *news media*.)

The news Websites most people visit are all online versions of traditional media. They are, in decreasing order of popularity: MSNBC.com, CNN.com, NYTimes.com, ABCnews.com, USA Today.com, WashingtonPost.com, Time.com, LATimes.com, FoxNews.com, and WSJ.com.

The hope that the Internet would spawn a galaxy of independent news sites has all but died—as the handful of corporations dominating the "old" media now dominate online, too. You can click and find plenty of alternative news on the Web, but realize that relatively few of your fellow citizens are logging on with you. (Nonetheless, you should take advantage of obscure news sites to reach target audiences.)

The big national news sites get most of their news from their well-known offline news operations. They mix their own pieces with content from news services, like the Associated Press, and stories from other media outlets with which they have partnership agreements. The sites are updated each morning, and breaking news is added during the day—mostly news service stories. Archived stories and resource offerings are available as well.

Like the Websites of the national media, the Web versions of your local news outlets are filled with content from the offline entity—with a smattering of original material produced for cyberspace, plus news service stories. For example, the Website of the *San Francisco Chronicle* is mostly composed of stories that appear in the newspaper. The Websites of local TV stations in San Francisco contain the stories that appeared on the air—in addition to news service copy and links to other Websites for additional information about different topics.

On occasion, a media outlet will "break" a story on its Website prior to its appearance on the air or in print.

Many news sites on the Web allow you to respond to articles online. Sometimes the articles are grouped together in broad topics, and you are given space to comment on the topic—or to respond to someone else's posted views on the topic. In some cases, reporters are available for "chats" online about selected topics.

Websites for General News

During the e-craze of the late 1990s, some media observers believed that online news sites would take over the news business, hiring top-notch reporters to produce stories and attracting advertisers and news consumers away from traditional news outlets. But the explosion of the Internet bubble sent many online news sites into oblivion, leaving a dearth of independent general news sites that have reporters on staff.

Two of the largest of the remaining sites are Slate.com and Salon.com. The sites both have original articles, including investigative pieces and commentary. Pitch them mostly as you would "offline" journalists, with short e-mails and crisp follow-up calls.

"My preview screen [for e-mails] is three lines, maybe about 20 words," says David Plotz, Washington editor of *Slate*. "That's about all you get of my attention."

You should provide online news outlets with material that is Web-friendly. After all, if you are reading news on a Website like *Slate*, you probably like trendy stuff on the Web. "We like reports with excellent online functions that we can link to," says Plotz. "One group opposing shipping nuclear waste across country issued a report with a map that allowed you to see how close it would come to your house."

Websites for Niche Audiences

While the largest online news sites don't have much original content, smaller news sites that target specific niche audiences may generate their own material—which they post on their sites and distribute via e-mail along with articles published elsewhere. You can find specialized Websites covering many causes, political issues, and news topics, from space (space.com) and women's issues (ivillage.com) to business (thestreet.com) and the environment (gristmagazine.com). Multi-issue political sites include alternet.org, mediachannel.org, and tompaine.com on the progressive side, and—for the conservative perspective—there's drudgereport.com, which is the widely known conservative site that broke the Monica Lewinsky saga, and other sites.

Contact reporters whose work appears on these types of sites or pitch the editors. Or you may be able to submit your own work. Offer them whatever they'll use—story ideas, previously published articles, news releases, reports, electronic newsletters, fact sheets, photos, whatever.

As with any PR endeavor, the key is to identify a news site on the Web that will reach your target audience, and figure out how to convince it to carry your story. For example, I once promoted a Web-based company that aimed to sell "peace flags" to people who—in the wake of the 9/11 attack—wanted to wave a flag but did not want to show the U.S. flag which, they argued, implied support for the invasion of Afghanistan.

The peace-flag makers' efforts to get their business off the ground were everything but peaceful. They received death threats and hate mail. Hackers attacked their Website, turning it into a pornography center. Flag manufacturers from across the United States rejected their business, and they were accused of being unpatriotic.

I managed to place a story about the travails of the peace-flag company in the *Los Angeles Times*. But because the people most likely to buy a peace flag were political lefties, not your standard Chamber-of-Commerce types, I submitted the published article to Commondreams.com, which posts daily news about politically progressive activities and opinion—the majority of it previously published elsewhere.

Testifying to the wisdom of finding your target audience, the peace-flag company sold many more flags after the *Los Angeles Times* article appeared on Commondreams.com than it did after it was published in the prestigious *Los Angeles Times*.

Keep in mind that only about 15 percent of U.S. citizens get their news online—and a disproportionate number of these people are white, wealthy, and young (most in their 30s). Over a *few days*, the network news shows have a greater combined audience than the total, combined monthly hits received by the top ten news Websites. This speaks to the importance of using the Internet strategically—just like any other communications tool.

News on Search Engines

Portals and search engines, Websites like Yahoo.com, aol.com, Excite.com, and Go.com, are popular sources of news on the Web. In fact, more people look for news on Yahoo than any other source online. A button on these sites, typically labeled something like "headlines" or "news," connects you with a list of top news stories of the day—all generated by wire services and other traditional news outlets. Staff at search-engine sites do not produce original reporting. Instead, editors select stories for placement on their Websites. You can lobby these "online" or "Web" editors to pick stories about your issue. To do so, determine who's in charge of updating the news page of these Websites. (Try e-mailing the webmaster or simply calling the company.) Then pitch the news editor via e-mail and phone.

But soon much of the work of these editors may be replaced by computers. Google updates its news offerings every fifteen minutes or so, using computer software to troll 24/7 for a selection of articles from thousands of Web news sources.

36

Media-Friendly Websites

JOURNALISTS LOOK FOR INFORMATION that's clear, without gratuitous frills, and is supremely understandable.

When it comes to your own Website, don't force journalists to wade through layers of obstacles (like unnecessary graphics and imagery) before getting to the information they need.

Much of this, it turns out, is similar to what anyone visiting your site might want. But to ensure a hassle-free experience by journalists, create an impossible-to-miss button labeled "media center" or "news room." Include in your news center, above all else, full contact information, including a street address and *phone number of a media contact* displayed prominently.

"It's irritating when you click on a 'contact us' button and it automatically brings up an e-mail," says Susan Ruiz Patton, philanthropy reporter for Cleveland's *The Plain Dealer*. "Sometimes I need to talk to someone today."

Also make sure your site's news center has news releases, with media contact phone numbers for each.

"The fewer graphics the better," says Janie Magruder, health and fitness reporter for the *Arizona Republic*. "I have a slow computer and I want the site to load quickly."

Tips for Creating a Media-Friendly Website

- For reporters, create a "media center," *easily* accessed from your home page, with 1) a snail-mail address and media contact's phone number, and 2) news releases, going back as many years as possible. Don't make journalists search around for this basic information. An e-mail contact is not good enough.

- Do *not* require a password for entry to your media center.
- Write minimal text for all pages, including pages in the media center.
- Your Website should have a dedicated page for news clips, including video clips, not only for journalists but all your site visitors. (Journalists should be able to access these clips from the media center.) If necessary, link to another Website that will host your video news clip and "stream" it for your site's visitors to view. (When you show video on a Website, it's called video "on-demand streaming.")
- Create a gallery of logos and photos and video of key activities. Again, journalists should be able to access these pages from the media center.
- Upload all fact sheets, reports, or any publication, including advertisements, annual reports (with financial information), brochures, newsletters, posters, flyers, and more.
- A search mechanism and site map are helpful, even if your site is relatively small.
- Brief biographies, titles, job descriptions, and photos of board members and key staff should be available.
- Remember that journalists like to print pages from Websites. Make sure yours are easy to print.
- Describe your organization, its history, and its activities in everyday language. Including a mission statement is fine, but often mission statements fail to communicate what an organization actually does.
- Label all sections of your site clearly.
- Keep your site current, and indicate when it was updated last with a phrase like, "last updated on June 12, 2003."
- Be realistic. For example, while it often makes sense to accept credit card donations on your Website, an on-line store can be a major headache for little or no gain, unless you've got a market to justify it.

Make sure reporters can find your site. To accomplish this, promote your site as if you were publicizing it for the general public. At the very least, convince other organizations to link their Websites to yours. This helps your site get noticed by search engines, like Google.com. Contact allied organizations first, and offer to link your site to theirs if they link their site to yours. You should consider hiring a consultant to promote your site on the Web. For free advice, see www.promotionworld.com.

Overall, be clear on how you want journalists to use your Website, and maintain it as such. Some sites are filled with the most current information about an issue, making them a constant resource for journalists. Other sites simply describe organizational initiatives and related information, and journalists only visit them when the organization is newsworthy for whatever reason. Either approach is fine, as long as you know which one you are using.

At a minimum, make your site easy to navigate. "It's almost as if some companies don't want you to know certain things," says Magruder of the *Arizona Republic*, when asked what was the most common problem on nonprofit organizations' Websites.

Ruiz Patton of *The Plain Dealer* advises nonprofits against including too much information and too many choices. "It's overload," she says, "especially when you are in a hurry."

Websites are definitely a great resource for journalists, who don't want to wait around for faxes, brochures, and even e-mails. Make sure yours works for them.

37

Bloggers

THANKS TO THE INTERNET, MORE people are skipping traditional news outlets—like newspapers, TV, and radio—and getting information from strange and fragmented sources.

One such source is "blogs" (a contraction of the words "Web" and "log").

Blogs are Websites that contain a stream of opinion by a Web pundit, called a "blogger." Though blogs do not have a single form, most are like diaries (Web logs), with frequent updates by the blogger. It's the perfect medium for someone who craves to give or receive nonstop opinions. One blog is appropriately named instapundit.com.

Blogs are chatty, confrontational, gossipy, snide, irreverent, and fun, with a generous offering of links to everything—allowing you to "see the proof" when a blogger trashes another writer or a public official. They offer a wider range of opinion than you find in the establishment news media.

Some people find them unreliable, boring, and self-indulgent, which they certainly can be, especially because all people familiar with a computer can set up their own Website and proclaim themselves a blogger. But the gritty nature of blogs also makes them interesting. If the sterility of most corporate media bothers you, you may like blogs.

As Judith Shulevitz wrote in the *New York Times*, "Blogs are the antidote to the blow-dried anchor and the unsigned editorial."

Hundreds of thousands of blogs grace the Web's blogosphere. You can find them on any topic. Some have weird themes like www.popculturejunkmail.com, which covers "trashy TV, British Royalty, the 1980s, toys, movies, cats, weird makeup, and more." Some have no definition at all. Others focus on politics.

Most are founded by type-A personalities with time on their hands and free of any connections to media conglomerates. The blog phenomenon took off in the late 1990s when it became easy for regular people to create and update Websites. The software's free. For an example of free software, see www.noahgrey.com/greysoft/.

As the blog trend has gotten more press attention, traditional media outlets have begun to add blogs to their official Websites. For example, MSNBC.com has seven bloggers.

Is it worth trying to inject your message into blogdom? If your target audience likes blogs, then yes.

"There's only one way to do this, and that is to know what your hook is," says blogger Eric Alterman, whose "Altercation" blog can be found on www.msnbc.com. "You need a hook that matches the [blogger's] interest."

Tips for Getting the Attention of Bloggers

- Be highly selective in choosing your target blog. Most are read by no one except the blogger and his dad or mom. Find blogs that are well-known.
- Connect your issue to the theme of a blog. Blogs can connect you to a well-defined audience with an interest in a specific topic or with a definite political leaning.
- Use blogs to reach an elite audience. Respected blogs attract trend setters and journalists themselves, making them useful if you are trying to communicate to this hard-to-reach audience. In this respect, they are quite different than chat rooms, which are used by informed citizens, but not the opinion-forming crowd that will bookmark a blog.
- Monitor targeted blogs or use blog search engines that search blog content. See www.blogcritics.org, or a search on Google.com will yield a breakdown of blogs in numerous categories.
- Talk back to bloggers; inject your issue whenever possible—and do it quickly. This is the best and easiest way to

break into blogs with your cause. Many bloggers liberally share comments—but they don't post everything.

"It's like a cocktail conversation," says Alterman, msnbc.com's blogger. "If you come in and interrupt with your cause, you'll be ignored. I want letters to have something to do with issues already on the web log."

38

Viral Marketing

VIRAL MARKETING IS THE Internet-age equivalent of promotion by word of mouth. The difference is, it relies on e-mail, not your chops, to spread the word. So it's much more efficient—unless you've got the status and mouth of someone like Bill Clinton. Here's how it works:

You get an e-mail with a political joke, information about a rally, a funny photograph, or whatever. You compose a little note like, "Check this out," and forward the e-mail message to a dozen people whom you think would like it.

Your contacts receive the e-mail from you, and they forward it to their friends, and so on, spreading the e-mail message like a virus from one computer to another.

Viral e-mail works because each e-mail that's passed on carries the personal endorsement of whoever forwarded it. Because the viral e-mail comes from a person known to the recipient, he or she will most likely pay attention to it—unlike typical unwanted and anonymous e-mail, called spam, which lands in your e-mail box and you delete without reading. In short, an e-mail forwarded from a friend has legitimacy.

Not surprisingly, it's much easier to create *non-political* e-mail that catches people's attention than an e-mail with a political message or one that *encourages folks to take political action.*

"Frog Blender" is an example of a *non-political* viral e-mail that was a hit. This was an e-mail with a link to a Web-site where you played a game called, yup, Frog Blender. It featured a green frog floating in a blender full of water. The frog said, "What are you looking at? What? You ain't got the

231

balls . . ." The swimming frog repeats this, as you read the instructions telling you how to start the blender, which you do. On low speed the frog just spins slowly, but at high speed it is completely pureed. That is, if you have the guts to push the button on the blender.

Frog Blender was passed on to countless people staring at computers.

You can make life meaningful for these bored people by developing viral e-mails for political causes. The e-mail messages can simply spread the word using text—as in "Please come to our rally. . . . Pass this on."

You can "embed" photos, art, or graphics directly in a viral e-mail to wake up your recipients when they open it. Your viral e-mail can also link to a Website where you play a game, like Frog Blender. The options are extremely wide—and they multiply every day as Internet technology develops.

Viral e-mails can include an "action" step, which means they can allow recipients to e-mail or fax their politicians with the click of a mouse. Or they can include a link to a Website with everything you need to take actions large and small.

Your viral e-mails can allow people to sign up to receive future action alerts by e-mail. You should read the previous sentence again because it is so important. As you will see in some of the examples below, it's possible to build a powerful organization, with hundreds of thousands of members, and raise millions of dollars, based on the strength of a single viral e-mail.

It's way hard to create a successful viral e-mail, but that doesn't mean you shouldn't try to come up with something that breaks through.

Examples and Classification of Viral E-Mails

Petitions

You wouldn't think that a simple e-petition, launched by e-mail at the right time, could change your life, but read this story: Wes Boyd and Joan Blades were sick of the Clinton impeachment trial—like the rest of the country. So they put their computer backgrounds to work to do something about it. They created a Website called MoveOn.org with one refreshing wish on it: "Congress must immediately censure the President and move on to pressing issues facing the country." With a click of a mouse, visitors to the Website could zap the message to Congress—and they did. Five hundred people did it the first day. Then 1,500 on the second day. On day three, the number increased to 9,000. It hit 100,000 in one week. The Website address was e-mailed to hundreds of thousands of people. When the House voted on impeachment, MoveOn.org was up to 300,000 responses.

Later, MoveOn.org raised over $2 million from its petition signers to unseat impeachment-crazed legislators and over $4 million for progressive candidates in the 2002 election. The organization has focused on campaign finance reform and the Middle East crisis, among other issues, offering people an easy way to make a difference. During the months before the Iraq war, MoveOn's membership skyrocketed, exceeding one million people in the United States and an additional million abroad. Over the years, MoveOn's alerts have urged members to meet with their elected officials, write letters to the editor, attend vigils and rallies and call, fax, or e-mail their representatives.

Photos

Someone e-mailed me a link to a Website with beautiful photos of orangutans. Why spend time looking at orangutans? Ordinarily I wouldn't, but I checked out the site because I knew the sender— and it turned out the apes were amazingly human-like and startling, especially if you've been sitting at a desk all day. I forwarded the message to some people, including my mother—and she sent it to others. But who cares about photos of orangutans? Well, the Center for Orangutan and Chimpanzee Conservation does. And I was looking at their Website thanks to a simple photo.

Joke photos are effective, like the one I got recently of President George W. Bush reading with a young girl—with the preamble to the Constitution in the background. Bush's book is upside down, while the girl's is right side up. Who knows if the photo was real, but it was still funny.

You can set a group of photos to music to add drama, humor, or emotional pull.

Animations

You can create short animated cartoons with messages. Most often they can go to a Website. In either case, these clips should not run more than a minute or so. Mark Fiore has created animations for political organizations. In a recent piece, titled "Special Ops," stealth music plays as "John Ashcroft and federal agents are on the job . . . protecting America from the sick & dying." At the conclusion of the cartoon, a group of people are sick in bed holding a "Yes to Medical Marijuana" sign. See more examples of animations at www.blah3.com, www.dubyadubyadubya.com, www.markfiore.com, and www.miniclip.com.

Celebrity Endorsements

Robert Redford has worked extensively with the Natural Resources Defense Council (NRDC) on various environmental issues. NRDC distributed a simple letter from Redford when President Bush's proposal to drill in the Alaska National Wildlife Refuge was in the news. The subject line on the e-mail indicated that it contained a letter from Robert Redford. It was launched to about 30,000 people and recruited over 100,000 members for NRDC.

Games

Once I got an e-mail that allowed you to select various animated weapons to drop on President George W. Bush. This was overly violent and probably illegal, so I thought of a less violent, and more juvenile, approach—spanking the president—that was later used by a client, TrueMajority.com. It produced an e-game called SpankBush, allowing viewers to engage in a new, *hard-hitting* form of Democratic expression: spanking the hindquarters of the president. Visitors to the SpankBush.com Website choose from among sixteen reasons for the spanking. The reasons include: "war on Iraq," "tax breaks for the rich," "mangled English," "environmental disaster," and "lone ranger." Then visitors are asked to choose an instrument for the spanking—either a fish, a paddle, or a hand. As the spanking proceeds, the president makes various cries for help, including, "Jeb, brother, I need you again," "Daddy," and "Evildoer." After the spanking is completed, visitors can send their spanking to the White House with a letter that reads, in part: *I hope that after I spank you, and the sting subsides, you will pull up your pants, look in the mirror, and resolve to be a better President.*

TrueMajority.com uses e-mails like this to recruit members. The TrueMajority's e-mails are forwarded virally, and recipients are urged to sign up for the TrueMajority for free. The aim is that people get sufficiently inspired by the viral e-mail and become a member of the TrueMajority. For example, over 5,000 people joined the TrueMajority after visiting SpankBush.com. Those who join receive free monthly action alerts. By clicking on a link in the monthly e-alert, TrueMajority members generate a fax to their congressperson, the president, or others.

Other e-mail games include: www.greedytv.org (about campaign finance reform), www.georgewbuy.com (about Bush forest policies), and www.whackaflack.com. (about the PR industry).

Again, the best games are not only on message, but lead players to a political action.

Tips for Creating Viral E-Mails

- Design your e-mail around what's on people's minds. Use news hooks, as you would if you were pitching a news story to the media.
- You can focus on viral e-mails requiring little or no money—and do it yourself. To create more complicated and expensive viral e-mails, like animations, you will probably have to work with a techno-savvy consultant like Konscious Media (www.konscious.com) or CTSG (www.ctsg.com).
- Assume all your recipients have dial-up modems. Don't send e-mails that will take a long time for people with dial-up modems to receive.
- Keep it short. All your Internet communication should use short sentences, short paragraphs, and short everything.

- Give careful thought to what you write in the subject line of your e-mail.
- Virals should offer folks an action step—in addition to delivering a political message.

Getting News Coverage of Viral E-Mails

Many of the above examples of successful viral e-mails got media attention, which helped both the cause and the organization. Essentially, they became trendy enough to be newsworthy. (Even if they do not make the news, they can be powerful forms of *independent* media, not relying on the news media to spread the word.)

You'll have the best luck at getting coverage of your viral e-mail if it's fresh and connects to current issues. The tactic of using an e-mail petition, for example, is now sort of passé—but it could still work at the right moment.

It's also helpful if you can document for journalists that your Internet campaign is having an impact. This means you should try to track anything quantifiable about your viral e-mail: How many e-mails, faxes, or calls did it generate? How many members signed up for your organization as a result of the e-mail? How many times have people received it?

The sooner you jump on an emerging issue, the more likely you are to get coverage. For example, as the California energy crisis worsened, a "rolling blackout" e-mail—suggesting that citizens turn off the lights at specific times in support of energy conservation—got major coverage in western states.

The Internet is a godsend for activists with a lot of passion but little money. Viral marketing epitomizes the low-budget, high-impact potential of the Internet.

Part SIX

Prime-Time Guerrilla Activism

IF YOU'VE GOTTEN THIS FAR into this media guidebook, you must have some guerrilla blood in you. You're not the type who wants to sit at a desk and crank out news releases. You're at least interested in, if not committed to, taking risks and confronting misguided and evil people and institutions. You don't want to waste your life being passive.

This section will give you some ideas on how to translate your guerrilla leanings into serious action—beyond the news-making tactics that I've already covered. (See Part One, "Stop Being a Bore.")

As you read this section, think of the motto of the Ruckus Society: "Action Speaks Louder than Words."

39

Civil Disobedience and Surprise Protests

Nonviolent direct action is for people who want to make change happen today, through intervention, civil disobedience, or other tactics that focus on immediate results. This isn't just for lawless freaks. If it were, Mahatma Gandhi wouldn't be an international hero and Martin Luther King Jr. wouldn't have a national holiday in the United States named after him. Civil disobedience is a respected tool that activists use when they feel they must break the law—and when they are prepared to pay the possible consequences of jail time, fines, personal injury, and community disrepute.

It also gets attention. "I wouldn't encourage people to get arrested," says Greg Todd, a former editor for the *Rocky Mountain News*, "but that definitely adds to the news value of the story."

Media attention should be an integral part of nonviolent direct action—as long as you are clear that the tactics you are using will advance your goals. News coverage expands the audience of witnesses to the injustice that's being opposed. And nonviolent direct action has a long history of working. For example, even if you disagree with those of us who protest at international gatherings—like meetings of the World Trade Organization, the G–8, or the World Bank—you have to acknowledge the impact. After the protests in Seattle, the economic leaders of the world put debt relief for developing nations and special funds to fight AIDS, tuberculosis, and malaria higher on the agenda—at least raising the profile of these poverty issues. The complexities and fairness of global trade were debated across the media landscape, ranging from the front page of *Newsweek* to network TV. While it's true that the tactics—particularly the property destruction by a few—turned off many people, the issues emerged through the clutter.

Preparing to promote an act of nonviolent direct action is similar to organizing any media event (See Part Three, "How to Stage a Media Event.") The major difference arises when you alert journalists to your event. This requires careful planning, because the success of many actions relies on surprise. For example, if activists want to climb ancient trees to protest illegal logging, they must have access to the forest. If it's announced in advance that the activists are coming, officials may deny them access, effectively nixing the demonstration. The same surprise element was critical in the following actions involving civil disobedience, all of which received substantial media coverage.

- More than 150 members of a group called Homes Not Jails broke into a former military base and occupied vacant military homes in San Francisco, calling on the government to convert the homes into low-income housing;
- A small band of fair-trade activists, dressed in formal wear, infiltrated a gala thrown by the Toronto mayor for a trade group representing multinational corporations. They left parcels filled with rotting eggs and fart bombs. Free Trade Stinks. Literally.
- First heckling then blowing whistles, members of the ad-hoc AIDS Drugs for Africa disrupted Al Gore's formal announcement that he was running for president. They were eventually escorted out by police.
- A protester flung a rotten salmon at Congresswoman Helen Chenoweth-Hage, Republican of Idaho, during a hearing on forest health. The hearing recessed while the congresswoman wiped the salmon from her hair and jacket.
- Activists with the Barbie Liberation Organization switched the voice boxes of Barbie and G.I. Joe dolls on sale at a toy store. Dressed in army fatigues and clad with machine guns and grenades, the G.I. Joe doll said, to the astonishment of

the shopper who bought the item, "Want to go shopping?" and Barbie said in a deep voice, "Dead men tell no lies."
- Continuing a tradition pioneered in the 1960s, the Biotic Baking Brigade (BBB) threw organic pies in the face of public officials and wrongdoers—an activity the brigade called "entartments." Members have struck San Francisco Mayor Willie Brown, economist Milton Friedman, World Trade Organization officials, Bill Gates, and others, generating international media coverage. Baking Brigade activists have served prison sentences, but believe that ". . . justice has not been served, which is why we serve up delicious mischief in the first place."

Tips for Alerting Journalists to Direct Action

Choose the Proper Location and Time, Compile a Media List, and Write a News Release

Like any demonstration, a surprise protest—like an act of civil disobedience—should communicate one simple message, which should be reiterated on any signs, banners, or flyers prepared for the event. Similarly, the image of your protest—for example, of homeless families huddled in vacant housing—should be crafted to help communicate your simple message. Ideally your image should communicate your message without any verbal explanation.

Again, follow the regular principles of good media work. Your event, if possible, should occur earlier in the day (between 10 A.M. and 3 P.M.) and earlier in the workweek (Monday through Thursday)—unless you want to try for live TV coverage in the evening.

Update your media list a week or so before your event. If your event will take place outside of regular business hours, make sure you've got the direct line to the news desks, and make sure someone is stationed at the news desk around the clock. If not, plan accordingly.

Your news release should be no more than one page with a dynamite headline and first paragraph. If you e-mail your release, you should paste in digital photos, if you have them, and state whether video is available. Here is the headline and first two paragraphs from a news release about an act of civil disobedience that occurred in Los Angeles.

Burmese-Americans Block Unocal Truck
To Protest Company's Pipeline Project
[Video available.]

A family of Burmese refugees chained themselves to a Unocal gasoline tanker early today to protest human rights abuses and rainforest destruction linked to construction of the LA-based company's southern Burma pipeline.

Dressed in traditional sarongs and holding their 4-year-old daughter, Maung and Taw Myo Shwe locked themselves to a truck leaving the Unocal Los Angeles Terminal Motor Transport facility at 13500 S. Broadway. They were joined by environmentalists from the International Rivers Network and other groups, who hung a large banner reading, "Unocal Stop Supporting the Brutal Burmese Regime."

Reporters interviewed these activists immediately after they were arrested—as police led them to a waiting paddy wagon. Advance practice helped the activists stay on message during this brief interview.
Credit: Jason Salzman

Assemble Your Press Kit

It should consist of about five pages of background material, including a CD with digital images, neatly organized in a folder. It's a good idea to have a separate fact sheet for distribution to the public, especially if you are engaging in civil disobedience in a public place.

Arrange to Have a Photographer and Videographer at the Event

Sometimes, if you fail to get journalists to attend your demonstration, you can later persuade them to accept your photos or video of it. It's especially important to have your own photographer if your event will take place outside of normal business hours—or at a remote location. Powerful news services like the Associated Press will accept photos occasionally. And broadcast outlets, including national and local news, may accept or even buy your video if it's good.

You'll have a better chance of success if your photographer has some professional credentials as a freelancer, but this is not essential. For example, in British Columbia, activists failed to draw any media to their protest of the logging of the temperate rainforest. Their demonstration involved blocking a logging road with concrete barrels. Workers from the logging industry vandalized cars, yelled at activists, chopped down a tree, and even started a fire near one activist who had chained himself to a barrel of concrete. Fortunately, the activists had a freelance videographer with them to tape the protest. After the event, the activists brought the film to local TV stations and received substantial—and lengthy—coverage on the evening news. The footage was accepted because it was so dramatic, showing the confrontation between the loggers and the activists.

Contact Trusted Journalists in Advance

You'll probably get better media coverage if journalists know about your protest in advance, allowing them to plan to be on the scene. However, tipping off journalists is risky even if you tell them not to divulge your story to anyone in advance.

Journalists may violate the "embargo" on your event, write a story about it, and thus undermine your protest. Or a journalist's editor might hear about it and alert the people you want kept in the dark. (A journalist might call someone from the opposing side for a comment on your upcoming event, inadvertently divulging your plans.) You never know.

Your best bet is to give advance information about your secret protest only to journalists whom you trust as professionals—and who will likely attend your demonstration. If possible, ask other activists for names of trustworthy journalists. Call them and explain what's going to happen, where it will take place, and why you are asking them to keep it secret.

Depending on the complexity of your protest, you may decide to meet reporters at a specific location and lead them to your demonstration from there. If you do this, be on time.

You may also decide—given the circumstances of your protest—to give advance warning to some reporters whom you do *not* know. One reason to do this: Your demonstration is in a remote location, making it impossible for them to get there on short notice. Another reason: You have to transport journalists on a boat or airplane to enable them to view your protest.

If you must tell unknown journalists in advance, call them directly if possible. If not, call city editors at newspapers, assignment editors at local television stations, producers at national TV shows, and news directors at radio stations.

Some activists opt to tell a larger number of journalists in advance that they have a protest in the works, without telling them the details or location. This helps journalists with planning, but it can be irksome to a reporter to receive partial information. I wouldn't recommend it unless your organization has an excellent track record.

Contact Journalists When the Action Begins

In an ideal surprise protest, a few trusted journalists are on hand the instant your demonstration starts. You can contact more journalists by fax or e-mail and phone once the action begins.

Station one person at the protest site and another in an office with a couple of phone lines, a computer, and a fax machine. Once the action begins (for example, activists have dropped a banner from the Statue of Liberty), your on-site person serves as on-the-ground media contact, while the office person faxes or e-mails your press release to all the reporters on your list, and makes follow-up calls by phone. Your on-the-ground person should get your office person a digital photo of the event as soon as possible.

Try to speed up the distribution of your news release. Load your media list into your fax machine or computer in advance. It may be worth it to hire a service that will distribute faxes simultaneously to many journalists rather than your having to send them in succession. U.S. Newswire or Bacon's Information, Inc., provide this service. Any way to distribute your press release faster should be employed.

If you send faxes one at a time, prioritize the contacts on your list. Generally, wire services and television stations should be contacted first. But as with all media work, this depends on the audience you want to reach. Do your prioritizing according to which media outlet will best reach your target audience.

Call all journalists to make sure they've received your press release. These calls are critical and should be practiced in advance. Get right to the point, emphasizing the drama and imagery of your demonstration.

Sample Call to a Journalist from a Protest Involving Civil Disobedience

Journalist: Associated Press.

You: I'm calling to let you know that two activists have just climbed the Sears Tower and dropped a huge banner down the side of the building that calls for an end to the death penalty. They're about 200 feet up the side of the Sears Tower right now.

Journalist: Do you have anything in writing?

You: I've just faxed you a press release, but I wanted to let you know that the protest is happening now at the Sears

Tower. Did you receive the news release? I can e-mail you a photo, if you want.

Journalist: I'll check. . . . Yes, I've got it. Can I reach you at this number?

You: Yes. Are you going to come down?

Journalist: I'll have to see. How long are you going to be there?

You: The police could remove us at any time. I'll keep you informed as the day goes on.

Journalist: Thank you.

Move through your list, making calls as quickly as you can, and then update journalists as the event proceeds. If major developments take place (confrontations, arrests, and so on), call key journalists again with updates. But don't pester anyone. If they don't sound interested, let them go quickly. Send them the release again, if necessary.

If you have time, you can phone outlets repeatedly by calling the "news tips" phone number and pretending you are a passerby who is amazed by the action.

Use cell phones to call talk-radio programs from the action site. This live communication makes great radio news.

Journalists may want to know about newsworthy antics used to avoid arrest. Once a woman was about to be arrested in Nevada by a mean-looking cop. She quickly stripped naked. The cop wouldn't touch her and called a female officer. Another activist defecated in his hand, which understandably sent the authorities running.

Dramatic protests do not always make news. In Chicago once, I was on a cell phone explaining to a television assignment editor at a local TV station that Greenpeace had two activists holding a banner on the side of a major hotel where nuclear power promoters were meeting. I said that the fire department was about to extract the activists from the side of the hotel. The fire truck had pulled up and the ladder was being extended toward the building. I asked the assignment editor if she was going to send anyone down. She said, "Call me if there is any blood or signs of police brutality." Clearly, local TV news in Chicago is tough to crack. But this protest would have been covered in most U.S. cities.

If your protest lasts days or weeks, expect coverage to accumulate over time. Don't get discouraged if you initially get no coverage. Your protest can provide a visual image for news that breaks while you're there.

When your demonstration ends, call all journalists who attended or expressed serious interest. Tell them what happened and where you can be reached during the rest of the day. If possible, conclude your protest with the media in mind. Sometimes you will want to negotiate an arrest scenario with police. If so, settle on a time for your arrest to coincide with live TV or before deadlines.

Finally, if you do get arrested, call journalists from jail. Talk-radio shows, in particular, are receptive to putting you on the air live from jail. (Plan for this by writing the phone number of media outlets on your body in case your clothes and belongings are taken from you.)

Sample Interactions with Media at an Event Involving Civil Disobedience

Sometimes during an act of civil disobedience, you will have time to answer only one question from a reporter. Your opportunity to deliver your sound bite may come as police are leading you to their patrol car and reporters converge on you.

Journalist: Why are you here?

You: I'm here to call on the U.S. government to ban mahogany imports.

Journalist: How do you go to the bathroom up in that tree?

You: Using diapers is inconvenient, but logging our old-growth forests would be a horrible tragedy.

Journalist: Do you have a job?

You: My job today is to alert citizens that the tobacco industry is killing our children by addicting them to cigarettes.

Journalist: Are you from this area?

You: It's everyone's responsibility to stop drunk driving.

Journalist: Do you care about putting workers out of their jobs?

You: We will have more jobs—and we'll save our forests—if we switch to tree-free products.

Activist Nadine Bloch recalls walking across the country as part of the Great Peace March, which advocated nuclear disarmament. A reporter asked how her feet were holding up. She said, "It's *not* about feet. It's about arms—nuclear arms."

Reporters will not focus exclusively on designated spokespeople at an event. They want other "unpolished" points of view, which is fair enough. Everyone involved in an action should be prepared to talk to a reporter. Some people may prefer to answer one or two questions and then tell a reporter to find the spokesperson.

40

Street Posters

"Wheatpasting" or "Wild Postering" has an honorable history in revolutions gone by, and the radical art form has a place in your revolution as well. Here's how to do it:

First, identify a target audience for your posters and develop a political message for them. Design a poster that will outrage, amuse, or otherwise engage these people. Try artists in your community. They usually appreciate the chance to help with political causes. The best posters are simple, with a big headline, colorful image, and guerrilla Website for further information, if possible. (Consider a Website registered overseas, but some wheatpasters have no worries about using a traceable Website.)

Then figure out where your target audience will see your posters. What part of town do your targets inhabit by day or night? What subway stops do they frequent?

Scout the areas where you want to poster and determine what size poster makes sense. For example, traffic-light switching boxes are great for hanging posters. Their size varies from city to city. Measure and plan accordingly.

A manageable general size is eleven inches by seventeen inches. Print on a light paper stock, recycled. Newsprint is best but not required.

Other possible targets are bus-waiting shacks, construction sites, telephone poles, dumpsters, deserted buildings, anywhere with a flat surface. Consider plastering a block of posters together for more impact.

How to Apply Posters

- Work at night on "vampire standard time," as the Lesbian Avengers suggest.
- Work in teams of three, if possible. One person brushes the wheatpaste glue (see recipe below), another slaps on the posters, and a third watches out for the authorities.
- Obtain a bucket for the wheatpaste, and a wide brush—like a wallpaper brush, sponge, or paint roller. See what works best for you. You may want a black plastic bag, which is easy to stash, to conceal your bucket and tools. I don't think gloves are worth the hassle.
- Brush a thin layer of wheatpaste *on the flat surface where the poster will be pasted.* Slap on the poster. Smooth it out. Some people brush a thin layer of wheatpaste over the poster as a topcoat, but you should *at least cover the edges and corners of your poster with wheatpaste so it can't be peeled off as easily.* (Most wheatpaste is fairly clear when it dries.)
- Make sure all corners of your poster are pasted down, and minimize bubbles or wrinkles. The posters are more difficult to remove this way.

Recipes for Wheatpaste

Like salsa, great wheatpaste can be made using various recipes. (In other words, this ain't no chemistry formula.) The easiest way: Skip the kitchen and buy it. Go to your local independent hardware story and purchase wallpaper adhesive, either in pre-mixed or powdered form. Mix the powdered stuff according to the directions—and then dilute it by two or three to one.

Home recipes for wheatpaste call for varying combinations of wheat flour and water. It's sort of like making gravy. (Wheat flour is regular old flour made from wheat. Use white or whole grain.) Here's a typical recipe: Mix one part wheat flour (for example, four cups) with three parts water (for example, twelve cups). Cook over medium heat until boiling, stirring constantly to remove all lumps. Lower heat and simmer for about a half hour. I never stop stirring. You will probably have to add water as it's cooking to get a substance that's smooth enough to use

Activists attached this poster to a lamppost with wheatpaste. It re-mained there for months. CREDIT: JASON SALZMAN

like paint but thick enough to stick to walls. Do not burn. Let cool before using.

You can also use cornstarch. Dissolve in cold water and then dump in boiling water to achieve the desired consistency. Apply when warm.

Postering and Media Coverage

You will maximize media coverage of your posters if you take responsibility for your work and actively seek out journalists, as you would for other events. (See Part Three, "How to Stage a Media Event.") You can try convincing a local TV film crew or print journalist to join you on your late-night cruise through town. Offer a reporter, preferably one you know, an exclusive to cover you.

But if you get in the news, you may face consequences (legal and monetary). For this reason, wheatpasters usually keep their identities secret.

Nonetheless, your posters can still get media attention. One obvious tactic to achieve this is to paste posters near media outlets—but avoid the appearance of pandering to the media by postering a large area.

Send copies of your poster, with an anonymous news release and follow-up call, to gossip-type columnists at local papers whose columns are filled with short snippy items, like the divorce of the local basketball hero or the upcoming charity event. Try alternative weeklies, local TV news, or—if you are attacking the business community—business reporters and publications. There's no formula for getting coverage. Try different angles, just as you would for any pitch.

Or you can incorporate posters into a multi-pronged action. In Chicago, activists dressed in shark costumes and paid a Sunday afternoon visit to the homes of key officials of a corporation practicing "predatory lending," which involves deceptively marketing overpriced and abusive home loans to residents of low-income neighborhoods. They plastered posters around the exclusive neighborhoods where the company executives lived—and around the company headquarters downtown. The posters read: "WARNING: Loan Sharks in Your Neighborhood."

"We've tried all kinds of actions against this company," said David Swanson, communications coordinator of the Association of Community Organizations for Reform Now (ACORN). "But this one got their attention."

Legal Considerations

Wheatpasting is not illegal in every city, but the rules—like having to take down posters—effectively make most poster efforts illegal.

So, arrange to have a lawyer available if you are popped. Some activists think the police won't arrest you for wheatpasting. Not true. Even before 9/11, New York City police arrested a friend of mine for wheatpasting small posters with the innocuous title, "The U.S. spends enough money on nuclear weapons to kill every child on earth, while 11,000,000 of our children go without health insurance."

Cops might just confiscate your gear, warn you, and let you go—even in the post–9/11 world. But arrests happen a lot, and you could face felony charges for property damage.

If you're stopped, do everything asked of you—including removing the posters—and you will have the best shot at avoiding jail.

If you're using a vehicle, make sure it works and that it—and you—are free of illegal substances.

P.S.–Kindness is central to saving the world. So don't plaster posters on houses or random cars—or anywhere they will obviously be a royal pain for everyday people to remove. (Some folks avoid government property.) Posters are really hard to peel off. If you hit the wrong target, help remove posters. Here's an e-mail that was sent around after a night of wheatpasting:

"Hey all–The wheatpasting around town has been a wonderful way to get info out, so it should definitely continue. However, the last time we wheatpasted, people must have accidentally wheatpasted someone's house in Cap Hill, and they need help removing the posters from the house. Whoever wheatpasted the house in Cap Hill, please call me to help clean the posters off the person's house. Kirby"

41

Spray, Stick, Cover . . .

In this world where commercial advertisements assault us everywhere, activists are often left with one viable choice: Execute an assault of our own that may not be bigger but is smarter, more aggressive, and more strategic.

Here's how to do it.

Billboard Alterations

Billboards are obvious targets for the guerrilla media activists. They're highly visible in public space and fairly easy to access. Billboard alterations, sometimes called billboard "corrections," are often covered by the news media, and if they aren't, your alteration still reaches a big audience who sees your work directly from the road.

One way to attack billboards is to alter them physically. The best method to do this is to find ads whose meaning is transformed by changing a single letter or word. So-called "Advertising Adjustment Activists" might change "Marlboro" to "Marlbore" or "Kool" to "Fool." "Got Milk?" is altered to read "Got Condoms?" "Channel 7 Stands for News" becomes "Channel 7 Stands for Lies." Billboards ads for cars are stamped with a large, "Cars Suck."

Unidentified activists recently pasted a "CANCELLED" banner over a giant billboard advertising the Ringling Brothers and Barnum & Bailey Circus. The action received major local media attention in Denver, including a large photo in the *Denver Post*. People for the Ethical Treatment of Animals (PETA), which campaigns against the circus, did not sanction the billboard alteration, but praised the message. This we-approve-of-the-sentiment-but-not-the-tactics response is a good way for an established organization to respond to radical protest. PETA actually offers a "canceled" sticker on its Website, urging people to use them creatively.

Another option is to occupy a billboard. Activists have climbed billboards and fasted. Or distributed paper-airplane flyers. Or done just about anything. Risking arrest atop a billboard adds drama to your story.

In one Greenpeace action that I promoted, activists climbed a Minneapolis billboard, which carried an advertisement for Northern States Power, a company known for its reliance on fossil fuels and nuclear power. The activists slipped a giant banner over the existing billboard. The banner asked, "Why Not Use Wind Power?" The activists perched on the billboard for one afternoon, landing an Associated Press photo as well has coverage by local TV news outlets and the *St. Paul Pioneer Press*.

Graffiti

Your "midnight re-decorating" need not be limited to billboards. Anything is vulnerable to graffiti—though this activity is not as newsworthy and can rightfully piss more people off. Using chalk for graffiti—instead of paint—is a kinder, gentler approach. In any case, think over the ethical questions carefully.

For political graffiti, you get the most impact if you can replicate an image as widely as possible. So, graffiti is often applied with a stencil, allowing you to rapidly spread the word on sidewalks, walls, or wherever. Simple images or phrases—like a radioactive waste symbol or "A Woman Was Raped Here"—work best. (You can cut a stencil from the reinforced bottom of a paper bag, making your activities less conspicuous and avoiding problems with wind.)

These days, even giant corporations use graffiti on occasion. IBM, for example, promoted the Linux computer operating system by spray-painting "Peace Love Linux" in Chicago and San Francisco. After an employee of a giant ad firm was popped by the cops, IBM fessed up and got a bunch of publicity.

Stickers

Carefully promoted sticker campaigns can get a lot of media attention. Take, for example, the group of activists who were concerned about the impact of SUVs on the environment—and fed up with the usual channels of protest. They chose bumper stickers as their weapons of choice and struck, sticking this message to the rear bumpers of SUVs: "I'm Changing the Planet. Ask Me How." Reporters found the www.changingthe-climate.com Website conveniently included on the bumper stickers. Website visitors can purchase stickers, make their own homemade bumper stickers, learn about global warming, chat, find out how to do it, and so on. The site also explains how owners of "tagged" SUVs can remove the stickers. The ad-hoc group, which has various chapters, received local and national media coverage, including National Public Radio, the *Wall Street Journal, New York Times*, Associated Press, and many others. (A page on the Website labeled, "Sue this Website," informs visitors, "error 504—due to very high traffic, the server is unable to process your request.")

In addition to stickers' potential for generating media coverage, they are also great at communicating to a specific target audience—whose location you can pinpoint. In one campaign I coordinated, we developed a sticker comparing the costs of schools and bombs, which we plastered in the men's and women's bathrooms at select events. We placed the stickers—which were statistical listings like a *Harper's* Index—on the walls of the bathroom stalls. Talk about communicating to a captive audience.

As usual, creativity with stickers goes a long way. To promote a new show on the Sci-Fi Channel, advertisers put 5,000 warning stickers on New York sewer grates: "WARNING: Spraying for Sewer Lizards To Commence Tonight. Take Appropriate Precautions." A Website listed on the stickers allowed visitors to find out "How I can protect myself and my loved ones." The hoax garnered national attention.

Parking Meters, Urinal Screens, and More

The beauty of stickers is that they are so easy to apply, and they can be sized to fit anywhere there's a gap in the advertising blitz that surrounds us. For example, I've seen guerrilla radio stickers plastered on the tops of parking meters, where people can't miss them. If your target audience is well-defined and small, you will probably be able to identify a strategic place where your audience is captive and a sticker will work.

Speaking of a captive audience, one activist group developed a "urinal screen" with a political message. For those of you—particularly women—who may not know, a urinal screen is the plastic screen at the bottom of a men's urinal. It holds the perfumed disk and stops trash from going down to the sewer, while allowing urine to pass through. The group's red urinal screens were printed with this message: "The Star Wars Missile Missed Its Target. Will You?" Gloves on, you simply walk into the bathroom, remove the old urinal screen, and lay down yours in its place.

Here's the anonymous news release that was distributed:

Star Wars Opponents Infiltrate Capitol Men's Rooms
Men's Urinals Targeted
Urinating Officials Face Question:
The Star Wars Missile Missed Its Target. Will You?

Even urinating government officials cannot escape from activists opposing Star Wars.

Men visiting the restroom during the during the Senate Appropriations Committee hearing on the Strategic Defense Initiative (Star Wars) were confronted with a stealth campaign . . .

42

Wrap Your Local Newspaper in a Fake Front Page

Viewers of Cincinnati's WKRC TV Channel 12 awakened to hear this odd story on a cold January morning:

> Well, some USA Today readers got quite a surprise yesterday. A group of peace activists wrapped some papers in a fake front page with the headline, "USA Decay." Officials with USA Today said they did not know how many street-side newspaper boxes were affected by this, but the group claimed to have hit boxes in nine different cities. . . . A group claiming responsibility wants money shifted from the Pentagon to education, healthcare, and the environment.

Like plastering posters to street posts, wrapping newspapers in a fake front page is a tactic that's been used by generations of activists who want to get the word out.

The concept is to create a fake newspaper front page that looks almost identical to the real thing. But upon closer examination, the fake front page turns out to have subversive articles, headlines, photos, and more.

You simply wrap the fake front page around newspapers in as many street-side boxes as possible—and let the news media know about it.

Guerrilla media activists wrapped USA Today newspapers with a fake "USA DECAY" front page. CREDIT: JASON SALZMAN

To pull this off, you need a graphic designer willing to mock up the dummy front page—and writers capable of producing engaging articles. Articles can be funny, serious, or both.

Once produced, the fake front page should be printed on newsprint, and sized to fold precisely over the real paper. In most cases, the fake front page should be a half sheet of newsprint with copy on one or both sides.

It's nearly impossible to wrap all the newspapers in street-side boxes in a city. So locate an area for maximum impact, like the central downtown district, including the area around media outlets, if possible.

The more activists willing to wrap, the more newspapers you can cover. Just a half dozen people can wrap a respectable number of papers—at least enough to get media attention. For tips on getting media attention for this activity, see the media section in Chapter 40, "Street Posters."

Ideally, wrap newspapers in teams of two with a vehicle. Wear clothes typical of a delivery person, like blue jeans and gloves, and make sure you've got plenty of quarters to open newspaper boxes.

Tips for Wrapping Newspapers

- Open a street-side newspaper box and remove the entire stack of newspapers from it. Place them in a container, like a cardboard box or plastic carrier, and bring the newspapers back to your vehicle.
- Inside your vehicle, wrap each newspaper in the fake front page and put the entire stack back in your container.
- Go to another newspaper box. Remove the wrapped newspapers from your container and place them on the ground.
- Open the newspaper box and remove the unwrapped newspapers, and place them in your container.
- Slide the wrapped newspapers into the empty newspaper box.
- Avoid police, but remember that this activity is so unusual that most authorities will never question you, even if you do it right in front of their noses. This is an illegal activity that is off their radar screens. Nonetheless, be sure to have a car that is properly registered and runs well. Also, discard all illegal substances.

Here are excerpts from the news release used by activists who wrapped *USA Today*:

Activists Wrap USA Today with Spoof Front Page
Newspaper Boxes Targeted in Nine Cities
Articles Lampoon Pentagon Spending and Call for Moving Taxes from Defense to Local Needs
Pick up a USA Today from a downtown newspaper box this morning—and you may think you need another cup of coffee.

Headlines in newspapers in nine cities read, "Defense, Education Departments to Merge," "Beating Plowshares into Swords," and "Pentagon to Throw Bombs Away."

The explanation? In a pre-dawn raid of street-side newspaper boxes, Shiftdough.org activists "wrapped" Thursday's edition of USA Today with a spoof cover sheet—so each newspaper had a fake front page with a "USA Decay" masthead. . . .

43

Guerrilla Activists
Hit Cyberspace

A MEDIA HOAX IS A NEWS story rooted in a lie. It's an event, business, Website, or anything that's presented to journalists as real, reported in the news as such, but turns out to be not true.

The trick is to invent a hoax that sends a meaningful political message—without alienating sane people everywhere. Hoaxes like bomb scares, fake computer viruses, or letters containing powdery white "anthrax-like" substances are nothing more than destructive. But there's another way to go. . . .

Pioneering media hoaxer Joey Skaggs has created both meaningful hoaxes and more anarchic ones—but his work has never crossed the line to sheer viciousness. Skaggs sees himself as an artist, an ethical liar with the news media as his medium of expression.

For example, he made a statement about political correctness with his widely covered campaign to "re-name the gypsy moth." Why? He claimed that real-life gypsies did not like the "gypsy" name used for a moth. This hoax included demonstrations by fake gypsies.

In another hoax, he advertised a "cathouse for dogs," which featured a "savory selection of hot bitches. From pedigree (Fifi, the French poodle) to mutts (Lady, the Tramp). . . . No weirdos, please. Dogs only. By appointment. . . ."

The stated purpose of the cathouse was not for mating but for the sexual gratification of dogs. Using actors posing as customers, he allowed reporters to view his cathouse, and got major coverage.

Website Media Hoaxes

The hoax discipline has boomed with the Internet. With a Website offering some amount of virtual legitimacy in the eyes of busy reporters, the possibilities for great political hoaxing have soared.

For example, Skaggs used a bogus Website as the basis for a recent media hoax satirizing the funeral industry. He set up a fake business called Final Curtain, which offered Walt Disney-like cemeteries for those who truly wanted to go out with a bang. He set up the Website and virtual office, with answering machine, stationery, and so on.

An article in the *Los Angeles Times*, which speculated that the business might be tongue-in-cheek, described Final Curtain this way:

> *Hoping to revolutionize the funeral industry, Final Curtain wants to build a chain of theme-park cemeteries featuring rides, shops, and outlandish tombstones designed by artists. The ideas for gravestones (which can be viewed at www.final-curtain.com) include a giant Etch-a-Sketch filled with cremated ashes mingled with iron particles . . . .*

Finally, in a parody of right-wing nuttery, activists established "Citizens Concerned about Barney," complaining that the famous purple dinosaur was leading kids to cocaine, gang violence, pornography, abortion, homosexuality, and drugs.

Look-Alike (Spoof) Websites

Instead of setting up an imaginary entity, you can create a fake Website that looks like the Website of your political target.

An example of this is www.gwbush.com, a parody of George W. Bush's official Website. It contains fake news about Bush and his White House adventures. Another site attacking New York

City Mayor Rudolph Giuliani was named www.YesRudy.com. This site was established in response to a Website set up by Giuliani to attack Hillary Rodham Clinton, then his opponent for the U.S. Senate. (If you want to parody a Website, think ahead and buy a domain name of a site similar to that of your political target.)

My favorite example of a fake Website is www.gatt.org, operated by Yes Men, an anti-globalization activist group. The site is designed to look like the official site of the World Trade Organization. In fact, it looked good enough to fool various organizations that wanted WTO speakers. They e-mailed www.gatt.org asking for Mike Moore, the WTO's director-general. Yes Men e-mailed a response saying that Mr. Moore could not attend, but another expert could speak. So posing as WTO spokesmen, Yes Man activists delivered lectures themselves! For example, in one speech the activists discussed how voting should be loosened up so corporations can participate more. In another lecture, the speakers defended the rights of slave owners and, while on stage, stripped down to a golden leotard and inflated a three-foot phallus. The WTO has denounced the Yes Men's deceptive Website—an action that resulted in more media attention for the Yes Men.

www.Dow-Chemical.com issued a fake Dow news release on the eighteenth anniversary of the Bhopal disaster explaining that Dow would not take responsibility for the disaster in order to maximize profits for its shareholders. The real Dow Chemical Company successfully pushed for the fake site to be shut down, generating wide publicity.

Hactivism

Hactivism is basically Internet geek activism. It can involve breaking into Websites and altering them for political purposes. For example, hactivists claim to have broken into the USA Today Website and added a story reporting that the White House had named a minister of propaganda. Hactivists have mangled corporate logos or ads and altered stories on news sites.

When the Chinese government blocked citizens from using Google to search for information on the Internet, hactivists in the

United States created a software program enabling Chinese Internet users to access Google through other portals.

Hactivists also devised a way to automatically divert mainland Chinese readers of a Hong Kong online newspaper to the Website of Falun Gong, which was outlawed as an "evil cult" by the Chinese government.

The hactivist's "virtual sit-in" involves flooding a targeted Website (like that of a bad corporation) with requests for information, which can temporarily paralyze or shut down the site.

Just like nonviolent direct action, all forms of "electronic civil disobedience" can be promoted to the news media anonymously or not.

The parameters of electronic civil disobedience are as wide as your imagination, but—like any kind of law-breaking—can result in severe consequences, even if you are doing it for a worthy cause.

Part SEVEN

Help, Media Frenzy!

Sometimes the tables are turned and journalists call on you without being beckoned. This attention can simply be a sign that your media work is effective: You're considered an expert—or your organization has been recognized as legitimate.

Sometimes you'd rather journalists go away. Part Seven provides information on how to deal responsibly with reporters when your organization faces a crisis that attracts them. It also outlines a process for you to handle routine—but unsolicited—calls from journalists who seek comments, data, or any other kind of information.

44

A Media Crisis

ANY NONPROFIT ORGANIZATION CAN FACE a disaster: Your delivery truck hits a pedestrian. Your opponents sue you, claiming defamation. One of your dinners for senior citizens is laced with poison. A sexual assault is reported in your building. Even if you think your organization is benign and powerless, serious problems can arise, placing you in the harsh light of the media. The rule in these circumstances is to release as much information as you can as soon as you can. This fosters a better working relationship between you and the media—and ultimately citizens. But release only information that you're absolutely sure is accurate. And make sure your release of information is legal and responsible.

"For us, the more open a group can be, the better," says Cathy Lawhon, team leader for the *Orange County Register*'s Lake Forest bureau. "Usually [groups] tend to circle the wagons and not give information at all . . . . If it's something that's sensitive, it seems to me that they'd be better off coming out with it and telling us their side of the story. We usually get the information anyway."

Prepare a Crisis Communications Plan

Even small nonprofits should develop a plan for dealing with the media in a crisis situation. At a minimum this plan should list a series of tasks to be completed when a crisis strikes (for example, who should be contacted, documents that should be prepared, specific issues that should be addressed). Then, when a crisis comes, you're far less likely to forget something.

At the heart of the crisis communications plans of many large nonprofits is a crisis communications team, consisting of—among others—the director of the organization, legal counsel, and the directors of public affairs and media relations. When a major crisis arises, these team members can think through the problem together and develop the proper response. At small nonprofits, unfortunately, the crisis communications team may consist of one person who performs multiple jobs—perhaps with consultation available over the phone. But in either case what's important is to make sure that all angles on the crisis are considered.

"Initially, there is quite often a schism between the attorney, who wants to say as little as possible, and the public affairs person, who wants to say as much as possible," says Alex Huppé, director of public affairs for Harvard University. But Huppé says differences can be minimized if staff take time to establish relationships and discuss the issues involved (for example, legal risks versus public relations) before a crisis arises. Huppé also points out that at larger nonprofits, media crises can be avoided by making sure that all staff know what's a crisis and what isn't.

Tips for Dealing with an Unwanted Media Frenzy

- Answer hypothetical questions with something like, "I don't want to speculate about that. I prefer to wait for the facts."
- Don't estimate or guess. Offer only confirmed, accurate information.
- Release as much information as possible as soon as possible. "Editors and reporters can get information that they think is true and build a story around it that could be far more damaging to the institution than the truth," says Fred Knubel, director of public information for Columbia University.

- Know what information you cannot legally release, and don't feel obliged to divulge all information, including proprietary or personal information.
- Always comment. In fact, as a media spokesperson, you should eliminate the phrase "no comment" from your brain. It makes you sound insensitive, elusive, and guilty. Instead, explain why you can't answer a question. A useful standby answer is, "I am gathering more facts about that issue right now and will respond as soon as possible." Other generic answers are "Our policy is . . . , and I am currently determining if our policy was followed in this case," or "My lawyer has prohibited me from discussing those details."
- Make sure it's clear whom journalists can contact for information, and make sure this person is available around the clock to take media calls.
- Don't get angry. (If you can't control your emotions, appoint a spokesperson who can.)
- The highest-ranking executive available should deliver as many statements to the media as possible in a crisis situation if he or she is a competent spokesperson. This adds authority, honesty, and sincerity to statements made in a crisis. (That's why all executives should receive interview training.)
- If your nonprofit faces frequent media crises involving government agencies (for example, the police) or other institutions, establish contacts with personnel at those external agencies.
- Allow plenty of opportunities for journalists to ask questions.
- Don't try to be humorous. It's not worth the risk.
- If you are confronted by reporters unexpectedly, don't walk or run away from the cameras. This footage will almost certainly be used.

Examples of Handling Media in a Crisis

Whether you're associated with a large institution or a tiny organization, your challenge in a crisis situation is to maintain clarity about what information you can legally and responsibly give to journalists while respecting their need for information. Know what you can say and how to get it out.

A Twenty-Million-Gallon Water Leak

"Emergencies always seem to happen at night or over the weekend," says Trina McGuire, media relations manager for Denver Water. "I got one call on the Friday afternoon before Memorial Day. A huge pipe that brought water from the treatment plant to the city had busted." By the time she got the call, businesses and a major interstate were flooded.

Journalists from all of Denver's major media outlets, who heard about the accident on police scanners, started calling immediately. All McGuire could tell them initially was that she knew the spill had occurred and that the broken pipe was owned by Denver Water.

McGuire made calls to her "crisis team," which includes—among others—key directors and managers from the legal, operations, and public affairs departments. She gathered information as quickly as possible.

"Within fifteen minutes, I called back the journalists and told them the size of the pipe and what it was. I told them it would be a while before we knew why it broke." One news outlet had falsely reported that 200 million gallons were lost when the actual spill was 20 million. She spent the next two hours making sure journalists had the correct information and relaying other information to them as she got it.

"We had relationships [with journalists] in place before this happened," says McGuire, allowing her, if necessary, to say with credibility, "This information is wrong." McGuire made sure that she got through to journalists she knew, rather than speaking to interns on the news desk, and that the journalists covering the spill could reach her around the clock.

As the crisis developed, some homes were flooded. "Because we were short-staffed, we didn't get to them fast enough," says McGuire. A few news outlets did stories about citizens whose homes were flooded and who were ignored by Denver Water. In response, Denver Water sent a group of employees to offer assistance to flood victims.

Says McGuire: "A bunch of us went door-to-door saying, 'We're from the Water Department. Is everything OK? Is there anything we can do?' We made sure the news media knew about it."

45

Unsolicited Calls from Journalists

As the nonprofit sector is subject to increased scrutiny by journalists and the public, nonprofit professionals need to be prepared to respond to probing questions even if they do not seek media coverage. You need to know how to deal fairly and effectively with journalists who call.

Your organization should have a plan to deal with press inquiries even if you choose not to seek them. You don't need a detailed plan, but at a minimum, train one or two people to respond to journalists. Also make sure that your organization's leadership has interviewing skills.

Tips for Responding to an Unsolicited Call from a Journalist

- One or two people in your organization should be designated media liaison(s) even if you don't have a communications department. Make sure they, at a minimum, read this book. Or better, they should attend a media how-to seminar.
- Make sure everyone who answers the phone knows that calls from journalists should be routed to your designated media liaison. (This does not mean, however, that others in your organization should be banned from speaking to

reporters. Journalists are rightfully skeptical if only a select few are allowed to speak to them. Anyone who wants
to speak to reporters should do so—if they are questioned.
Of course, this does not mean that everyone should *try* to
be interviewed.)

- Always take a reporter's call, but remember you can tell a
  reporter, once you speak with him or her briefly, that you'll
  call back.
- When a reporter calls, ask about the interview topic and
  format (live TV, phone, taped TV, talk radio, visit to the office, and so on).
- If necessary, tell the reporter you'll call back shortly. Remember deadlines. You want to prepare, but you don't
  want to miss a chance to comment on a story about your organization—even if it's a negative story.
- Make sure the journalist is actually with the news outlet he
  claims to represent. Call the main number of the outlet and
  ask if he's on staff.
- Determine who among your executive staff is available for
  interviews.
- If the reporter wants an immediate interview, quickly run
  through possible questions and answers with your
  spokesperson.
- Call the reporter back and work out the logistics of where
  and when the interview will take place. Or if it is to take
  place immediately, have your spokesperson call the reporter directly.
- Make a record of all unsolicited calls by reporters. Add
  names to your media list later.
- Your unsolicited call from a radio or TV journalist could be,
  essentially, an audition for a show: "If I were working for a
  TV station, I'd be interviewing you for information *and* au-
  ditioning you to see how you'd be on the air," says Peter
  Dykstra, a senior producer for CNN.

Sample Form for Recording
Incoming Calls by Reporters

Media Calls and Response Form

Date Call Received _____

Time Call Received _____

Name of Journalist _____

Title _____

Name or Call Letters of News Outlet _____

Phone _____

Fax _____

E-mail _____

JOURNALIST'S REQUEST:

DEADLINE: _____

Comments:

DATE/TIME REQUEST FILLED: _____

Logged in Media List: _____

Part EIGHT

Resources

Media How-to Books

Most large advocacy groups produce media guides about their issue for internal use. The guides are usually very helpful because they address the media nuances of specific issues. Ask a national organization that works on your issue if it has its own guide. In addition, you should supplement what you learn in this book by reading one or more of the following books:

The Jossey-Bass Guide to Strategic
Communications for Nonprofits (1998),
  Kathy Bonk, Henry Griggs, and Emily Tynes, Josey-Bass Publishers, San Francisco, Calif.

Spin Works (2000),
  Robert Bray, SPIN Project (www.spinproject.org).

Op-eds: A Cost-Effective Strategy for Advocacy (2000),
  Larry Kirkman and Karen Menichelli, editors,
  The Benton Foundation (www.benton.org).

Media How-to Guidebook (1999)
  Marianne Manilov, Media Alliance
  (www.media-alliance.org).

How to Tell and Sell Your Story (1997 and 1998)
  Timothy Saasta, Center for Community Change
  (www.communitychange.org).

The Practice of Public Relations (2001)
  Fraser P. Seitel, Prentice Hall, Upper Saddle River, N.J.

Conducting Successful Focus Groups (1999)
  Judith Sharken Simon, Amherst H. Wilder Foundation
  (www.wilder.org).

Making Money While Making a Difference:
How to Profit with a Nonprofit Partner (1999)
  Richard Steckel, Robin Simons, Jeffrey Simons, and Norman
Tanen, High Tide Press, Homewood, Ill.

News for a Change (1999)
  Lawrence Wallack, Katie Woodruff, Lori Dorfman, and Iris
Diaz, Sage Publications, Thousand Oaks, Calif.

Here are three good Websites: Gay & Lesbian Alliance Against
Defamation (www.glaad.org); Green Media Toolshed (www.
greenmediatoolshed.org); The Spin Project (www.spinproject.org).

Lists of News
Outlets and Journalists

The best way to obtain a list of journalists is from an allied organization that works on your issue. If this is not possible, Bacon's
and Burrelle's produce excellent media directories, but they're
expensive. (Or use them for free at a large library.) Free online directories lack the detailed information that you need, but they
can help you get started. (See Chapter 13, "Media Lists.")

Bacon's Media Directories (online, CD-ROM, or dead tree), www.ba-
  cons.com. The most expensive and best source.
Burrelle's Media Directories (online, CD-ROM, or dead tree),
  www.burrelles.com.
Capitol Advantage, www.congress.org. This is the best free online source. (Other free online sources include: www.cjr.org;
  www.newsdirectory.com; www.1america.com; www.news
  link.org.)

Guerrilla Media

The Web is full of wonderful sites with information about guerrilla action, like www.billboardliberation.com, www.rtmark.com,
www.sniggle.net, and many others. Surf and you will find. (See
Part Six, "Prime-Time Guerrilla Activism.")

The Activist Cookbook (1997), Andrew Boyd, United for a Fair
Economy (www.unitedforafaireconomy.org)
Wise Fool Basics (2001), K. Ruby, Wise Fool Puppet Intervention
(www.zeitgeist.net/wfca/wisefool.htm)
68 Ways to Make Really Big Puppets (1996), Sarah Peatie, Bread and
Puppet Press, Somerville, Mass.
Pranks (1987), RE/search (www.researchpubs.com)
Handbook for Nonviolent Action (1989), War Resisters League
(www.warresisters.org)
Adbusters Magazine (www.adbusters.org)
Ruckus Society (www.ruckus.org)

Media Monitoring

These three companies—among many others—will send you
"clips" when key words, like your organization's name, appear in the news (Web, broadcast, print). Beware: this can be
expensive.

Burrelle's Information Services (www.burrelles.com)
Video Monitoring Services of America (www.vidmon.com)
Luce Press Clippings (www.lucepress.com)

News-Media Watchdogs

These organizations direct citizen activism at the news media,
aiming to improve coverage and hold journalists to professional
standards.

Fairness and Accuracy in Reporting–FAIR (www.fair.org)
Rocky Mountain Media Watch (www.bigmedia.org)
Tyndall Report (www.tyndallreport.com)

Public Opinion Research

You can hire consultants to conduct polls or focus groups for
you. Or for much less money, you can mine existing data for information about public opinion about your cause. Here is a list of
existing sources:

Gallup Organization (www.gallup.com)
Pew Center for People and the Press (www.people-press.org),
    www.pollingreport.com
Program on International Policy Attitudes (www.pipa.org)
Roper Center for Public Opinion Research (www.ropercenter.
    uconn.edu)

More Resources

You can also search newspaper articles for free polling data.

For additional resources, check out my Website, **www.
causecommunications.com**. You'll find lists of PR consultants,
books, Websites, videos, and much more.

Index